# GREAT LEADERS

R. J. Unstead believes that the 'great leaders' in British history have made their mark on the story of Britain. He has chosen some of the most interesting leaders and reveals their characters—their weaknesses and their strengths—and the forces that motivated them.

3 bcd

Also by R. J. Unstead

THE STORY OF BRITAIN: BEFORE THE NORMAN CONQUEST
THE STORY OF BRITAIN: IN THE MIDDLE AGES
THE STORY OF BRITAIN: IN TUDOR AND STUART TIMES
THE STORY OF BRITAIN: FROM WILLIAM OF ORANGE TO WORLD WAR II
SOME KINGS AND QUEENS
ROYAL ADVENTURERS
PRINCES AND REBELS
DISCOVERERS AND ADVENTURERS

and published by Carousel Books.

# Great Leaders

R. J. Unstead

Illustrated by Ron Stenberg

CAROUSEL EDITOR: ANNE WOOD

**CAROUSEL BOOKS**
A DIVISION OF TRANSWORLD PUBLISHERS LTD
A NATIONAL GENERAL COMPANY

GREAT LEADERS

A CAROUSEL BOOK 0 552 54044 7

Originally published in Great Britain
by A. & C. Black Ltd.

PRINTING HISTORY
A. & C. Black edition published 1966
A. & C. Black edition reprinted 1967
Carousel edition published 1973



This book is set in Baskerville 12/13 pt.

Carousel Books are published by Transworld Publishers Ltd.,
Cavendish House, 57–59 Uxbridge Road, Ealing, London W.5.

Made and printed in Great Britain by
Richard Clay (The Chaucer Press), Ltd., Bungay, Suffolk.

**NOTE: The Australian price appearing on the back cover is the recommended retail price.**

CONTENTS

# ROBERT OWEN

Mr. Thickness, schoolmaster of Newtown in mid-Wales, stepped briskly into the saddler's shop.

'Mr. Owen,' he said, 'I am here to speak of your son, Robert.'

'Robert? I hope the boy has done nothing ill?' replied Mr. Owen anxiously.

'Nothing, nothing ill whatsoever. Indeed, all that he does is so exceptional that I propose, with your permission, to employ him to teach the younger children. In return, he shall have the rest of his schooling for nothing.'

'But Robert is only seven!' cried Mrs. Owen, coming in from the kitchen.

'So he may be, ma'am,' replied the schoolmaster solemnly, 'yet I declare that boy to be a little marvel!'

At that moment, the 'little marvel' himself ran into the shop.

'Robert,' said his father, 'do you think you could help Mr. Thickness to teach the other children?'

'I can beat them all at running and jumping, Father. Can I teach them dancing as well as reading?'

The boy spoke so eagerly that his words hardly sounded boastful. It seemed quite natural to him, as to everyone else, that he should be the best at lessons and sports.

So, at the age of seven, Robert Owen became a teacher. His group of children sat in front of him learning the alphabet and he was so patient and good-tempered that they tried extra hard to please him. Mr. Thickness noticed that the boy had a rare gift for making people listen to him.

But, at nine, Robert left school and went to work in a shop that sold drapery and grocery and, in his spare time, he read every book that he could borrow.

'At this time, I was reading a book a day,' he said later. 'I read *Pilgrim's Progress*, *Robinson Crusoe*, *Cook's Voyages* and all the lives of Great Men I could meet with.'

He had already made up his mind to be a Great Man. He was ten and it was high time to set off to London where his brother William was already in business as a saddler.

With a bundle of clean clothes and forty shillings in his pocket, Robert was put on the London coach:

'Farewell, Father!' he cried. 'Do not worry—I shall maintain myself and make my fortune presently!'

He spent a few weeks with his brother before receiving the offer of a job with Mr. McGuffog, linen-draper of Stamford. The offer was for three years with free food and lodging, no pay the first year, £8 the second and £10 the third.

Mr. McGuffog had built up such a high-class trade that every day six or seven carriages stood in line

outside his shop. For these genteel customers, the shop-hours were from ten until four and the whole business was conducted in a most leisurely, refined manner.

Young Owen became a favourite with his employer who taught him a great deal about best-quality fabrics and, after four years, he recommended him to Flint and Palmer, haberdashers, who kept a shop on Old London Bridge.

This was a very different business from Mr. McGuffog's. From eight in the morning till ten at night the shop was crowded with people turning over the huge stock of cottons and muslins in search of bargains. Business was brisk and the assistants were expected to be brisker.

'Don't waste time seeing that customers are satisfied!' cried Mr. Flint. 'Wrap up the goods, take the cash and serve the next lady!'

Robert had no regular meal-times; he just snatched a bite when he could and, after the shop closed, he had to sweep and tidy up before crawling into his attic bed.

He stayed there a year before applying for a job with Mr. Satterfield, a Manchester draper, who offered him the fine salary of £40 a year. He was now fifteen and had been keeping himself for five years.

In Lancashire, the great, booming industry was cotton-spinning. Robert saw factories for the first time. He went about and looked at new machines making new materials and he heard on every side that fortunes were being made. He also noticed that most of the workers lived in miserable poverty.

In this hard, go-ahead world, he kept his eyes open for the chance to become something more than a shop-assistant. He was eighteen when he met Mr. Jones.

Jones was a mechanic who supplied Satterfield's with wire-frames for ladies' bonnets, and when he called at the shop he would tell Robert about the spinning-machine he had made at home.

'Ah, Mr. Owen,' he said one day, 'you're a sharp young man. If only you and I had a little capital, we could set up in business together making machines.'

'I think my brother William would lend me £100,' replied Robert eagerly.

'Shake hands!' cried Jones. 'The firm of Jones and Owen is launched!'

With the borrowed money, they put up a workshop and engaged forty men to construct Jones's machines but Robert soon found he had made a poor bargain.

Jones had no notion of business and left everything to his partner who, in fact, knew very little about machinery. Owen did his best.

'I looked carefully at the men in their different jobs,' he said, 'although I really knew nothing. By observing everything with the closest attention, I kept the business going.'

Even so, the venture failed and Jones went off, leaving his partner nothing but five machines. Undaunted, Owen rented a big factory, and let off all the floor except one corner where he set up his machines. Then he hired three spinners and began to make yarn for the muslin trade. At twenty, he was an employer and he worked so hard that, within a year, he was making £6 a week for himself.

One morning, the men were talking about an advertisement in the paper. A Mr. Drinkwater was seeking a manager for a new mill, so Owen put on his hat and went round to Drinkwater's to ask for the job.

'You are too young,' said Mr. Drinkwater.

Robert knew that his fresh complexion made him look even younger than he was but he managed to brush this objection aside.

'What salary do you ask?'

'Three hundred pounds a year.'

'What? Several men want this post and all their askings put together would not come to £300.'

'I cannot help what others ask, for I cannot take less. I am making that sum in my own business.'

'Can you prove that?'

'Yes, I will show you my business and my books.'

Mr. Drinkwater was so impressed by what he saw that he offered him the post at the salary asked. Robert was to take complete charge of everything, including the 500 workers.

Astonished by his own boldness, he went along to the mill and walked round as though making a thorough inspection. He said not a word, apart from

'Yes' and 'No'. Years later, he confessed, 'After six weeks of watching and studying the workings of the machines, I felt so much master of my position that I was ready to give orders.'

Owen was so successful that Mr. Drinkwater raised his salary and promised to make him a partner after three years. But, when the time was up, he had to explain that because of company changes, he could not grant the partnership:

'I am anxious however to retain you as my manager at any salary you care to ask,' he added hastily.

Owen looked him straight in the face and answered:

'I have your agreement here. Look, I put it into the fire. But I will not stay as your manager!'

When word went round Manchester that the brilliant young Welshman had left Drinkwater, two wealthy firms offered to help him form a new company to manufacture yarn.

'But we will not compete against Mr. Drinkwater,' he told them, 'he was always good to me and I do not wish to injure him.'

As his business grew, Robert had to travel to various towns and sometimes to Scotland. One morning in Glasgow, he happened to meet two young ladies in the street and, although extremely bashful in the company of ladies, he felt obliged to raise his hat, since one was Miss Spear, daughter of a rich cotton-broker whom he knew. Miss Spear introduced her companion as Miss Caroline Dale, daughter of David Dale, the owner of New Lanark spinning-mills. Caroline liked the shy young man so much that she afterwards said to her friend:

'If ever I marry, there is my husband!'

But, for the moment, she invited Robert to visit her father's mills. This he did, not merely to see one of the biggest factories in the country, but because his mind was busy with plans that almost every other business-man would have considered crazy.

Ever since he had come to Lancashire, he had been troubled by the wretched condition of the workers. Many families lived in one room or in a corner of a cellar. They worked long hours yet their pay was so low that they took their children at five years old to earn a few pence mending broken threads or creeping under the machines to clean the wheels. No wonder that these mites were whipped to keep them awake. No wonder they died young or grew up mis-shapen, brutish and ignorant. Unlike other employers, Owen did not believe that workpeople were naturally dirty and lazy.

'I would change them into good citizens if only I could run a factory in my own way,' he said to himself.

The mills at New Lanark seemed to be exactly right for his plans. In his enthusiasm, he forgot his shyness and asked Caroline to marry him. She agreed, but he had still to persuade Mr. Dale to sell him the mills and to allow him to marry his daughter.

'I am by no means sure that I approve of that pushing young man from Manchester,' declared Mr. Dale.

But when Owen really wanted something, he could be the most charming, persuasive talker in the world. In the end, Mr. Dale gave in. He sold the mills to Owen and his partners and he permitted Caroline to marry the man she loved. On New Year's Day, 1800, Robert and his bride arrived at New Lanark.

The mills employed well over a thousand people but so many were needed that batches of orphans and foundlings were sent north from English workhouses. These tiny children had to work thirteen and fourteen hours a day, six days a week and for part of Sundays, in the hot, damp atmosphere of cotton-mills.

Mr. Dale employed 500 children and, although he treated them better than most masters, the situation filled Robert Owen with horror.

'Children so young should not be working from six in the morning until seven at night,' he cried indignantly. 'Many are dwarfs in body and mind. Some are deformed. Numbers continually run away and what can then become of them? Caroline, what can become of these poor children?'

As for the grown-up workers, they lived, he said, in wickedness and misery. And, for their part, they hated the prying Welshman who had come to live in the village, doubtless to squeeze more profit out of their labours. Owen was determined to turn these sullen people into good citizens. His first reform was to build an upper storey to their one-room hovels. He had piles of filth cleared away; the streets were paved and new homes were started. Finding that the wives were being cheated by rascally shopkeepers, he opened a company store that sold goods at fair prices and he bought coal by the truckload in order to re-sell it cheap.

Although the men did not like being punished for drunkenness and their wives were furious when Owen's 'Bug-Hunters' came to see that they kept their houses clean, they found that all the fines for misbehaviour went into a sick-fund and that Owen himself paid the doctors' bills.

In the factory itself, he put a stop to thieving and, to shame the slackers, he invented a device that he called 'The Silent Monitor'. A four-sided piece of wood was hung over each workplace. The sides were painted black, blue, yellow and white. Black denoted bad conduct, blue meant poor, yellow good and white excellent and the superintendent changed the tablets daily so that everyone could see who had worked well or badly. This childish scheme was a success because Owen realized that most of his workers, old and young, were no more than children.

The mills prospered. Owen's partners were delighted with the profits and the workers were better-off than ever before. Yet, because mill-owners were normally so hard, the men still distrusted their Boss. In 1806, a dispute between Britain and America stopped the arrival of raw cotton and, for four months, cotton-mills were closed and many workers were dismissed without pay. At New Lanark, Owen called a mass-meeting:

'Lads,' he said, 'there's no work for you until this trouble blows over. But it's none of your doing and, until the machines start up again, you shall all have your wages!'

It cost him well over £7000 but, from that time on, the workers trusted and adored him.

At heart, Owen was always a teacher and, after various set-backs, he was able to begin educating the children of New Lanark. He erected a large building that he called The Institute for the Formation of Character, and he insisted that every child in the village should attend from the age of one until at least ten, though he liked them to stay longer.

His ideas were amazingly modern. There was no cane and no timetable, for he believed that children ought to be happy and active in school. Lessons were often out-of-doors and he had paths cut through the woods to encourage the children to ramble and to learn nature study in the fresh air. There was singing and a kind of 'drill' with marching to fife-and-drum bands and, of course, dancing, in which Robert himself joined with the utmost gusto.

Above all, there was kindness. In his earnest, patient way he said to a young teacher:

'These children must never hear from their teacher an angry word. From the moment they arrive, you must tell them that the first aim of school is to try to make each other happy.'

His cherished plans were threatened when his

partners refused to pay out any more money for the school.

'I shall buy you out. How much do you want?' Owen said.

'Well, Mr. Owen, we can rely on you to name a fair price.'

'Eighty-four thousand pounds!' he snapped and the offer was gratefully accepted.

But, although he was growing rich, Owen did not have £84,000 and he had to find some new partners who, he believed, would allow him to run the business in his own way.

Unfortunately, they proved to be greedy and spiteful. They complained that he was too generous to the workers, that the school was a piece of high-flown nonsense, that they were in business for profit not for charity.

As before, Owen offered to buy them out.

'No, the mills must be sold,' they said. Secretly, they meant to buy New Lanark for themselves at a low price. Owen resigned and went away to London.

For a year, the struggle dragged on. Owen's enemies imagined that he was ruined, not realizing that he had found six wealthy admirers to support him. On the day of the sale, while Owen and his friends stayed in the background, their solicitor kept raising the price £100 above every bid until, at £110,000, the old partners could go no higher and the property was knocked down to Owen's supporters.

Straightaway, they set off by carriage to New Lanark but, about a mile from the mills, the London gentlemen were alarmed to see a huge crowd running towards them, shouting and hallooing. The horses were taken from the shafts and, heedless of the gentry's protests, the crowd seized the carriage and dragged it uphill to the village where the street was lined with cheering crowds.

'The mills are saved!' they shouted. 'Mr. Owen has come back!'

Robert Owen was to become world-famous, to travel all over Europe and America, explaining his idcas and founding new towns, schools and trade unions. Thousands of visitors were to come to New Lanark and he was to meet most of the distinguished men of his time. But in all the triumphs and disappointments of his long career, there was no happier day than when the people dragged his carriage into New Lanark and the children cried:

'Mr. Owen has come back!'

# WELLINGTON

'There he goes, that long-nosed beggar that beats the French,' remarked Private White of the 43rd, jerking his wine-bottle towards a spare, grey-coated figure who rode along the lines of resting soldiers.

'Aye, the Peer don't dress much like a general compared with them Spaniards and Froggies covered with blooming gold lace and medals,' replied Private Kemp, between mouthfuls of bread and meat.

'No, Kempy, but up and down this 'eart-break country, his long nose among us has been worth ten thousand men. He's beat all of Boney's marshals and he'll beat Boney himself one of these days.'

A bugle sounded. Orders to fall in were repeated down the line and Lord Wellington's soldiers, cursing as they eased on their 60-pound packs, resumed their march across the parched, biscuit-coloured land. Behind them creaked the bullock-waggons that carried food and ammunition for the army that was driving the French back to their own frontier.

As he rode with a single staff-officer, Wellington's mind was busy with tents, camp-kettles, blankets, wine and cloth. The muleteers and a Spanish guide had to be paid and compensation must be offered to a farmer whose barn had been accidentally set on fire.

The Commander-in-Chief saw to everything. He looked after his troops like a stern parent. He scolded and punished them, hanged a few for looting Spanish

homes, called them the scum of the earth and occasionally praised them as 'fine fellows'.

Today, he was in good spirits.

'Ned, I am going to hustle the French out of Spain,' he remarked to a staff-officer, pausing to scan the hills with his telescope. A distant movement caught his attention and he drew out one of the pieces of paper that he kept tucked in his waistcoat. He wrote rapidly and handed the note to a trooper:

'General Picton, on the right. Sharp!'

In his abrupt way, he gave orders:

'Light Division cross the river and get possession of the ridge.'

'Support the Light Infantry by Cavalry and Heavy Infantry.'

'3rd Division cross the road and take up such posts as you think proper.'

After four years, he had the French on the run and

he was not going to let them escape. Marshal Jourdan and King Joseph, Napoleon's own brother, decided to stand at Vitoria among the foothills of the Pyrenees and, as usual, Wellington left nothing to chance. He rode over the ground, studied maps and talked to local goatherds. Then he brought up his guns and troops to the exact position that he desired, knowing that the one-time rabble of convicts and runaways would not fail him:

'I could have done *anything* with that army,' he said proudly, 'it was in such splendid order.'

At Vitoria, the French fought hard but in the end they reeled back, groping for a way through the mountains, and Wellington followed them into France.

While the armies of Austria, Russia and Germany were massing against Napoleon, Wellington beat the French again, this time on French soil, and he was in the market-place of Toulouse when a colonel rode up from Bordeaux.

'I have extraordinary news, sir,' he said, saluting.

Wellington raised two fingers to his hat:

'Aye, I knew we should have peace. I have long expected it.'

'No, sir,' said the colonel. 'Napoleon has abdicated.'

'How, abdicated?' cried the Peer. 'You don't say so, upon my honour! Abdicated! Hurrah!'

To the astonishment of his staff, their ice-cold general spun round and round, snapping his fingers with delight as he performed a victory jig on the spot.

Arthur Wellesley, now Lord Wellington, had not always been the cool masterful hero. Sixth of nine children, he was regarded as the dunce of the family, and at Eton he made so little progress that his widowed mother Lady Mornington exclaimed crossly:

'I vow to God I do not know what to do with my awkward son Arthur. He wins no prizes at all. Really, he is fit only for gunpowder!'

She took him away from school to Brussels where the lonely unloved boy occupied himself learning French and playing the violin. Since the only place for a dull boy was the Army, he was sent to a French military college.

'If soldiering is to be my profession, I had better try to understand it,' he remarked drily.

Away from his mother and his brilliant brothers, he began to enjoy himself and to take an interest in military books and French ideas about war. His older brother Richard bought him a commission in the infantry, and at eighteen Arthur was an ensign in the Seventy-third.

For a time he served on the Staff of the Lord Lieutenant in Ireland where, during the round of parades, parties and balls, he fell in love with Lady Kitty Pakenham, an Irish peer's daughter. But it was hopeless to think of marriage on a junior officer's pay. Perhaps Kitty would wait for him.

'I will give up parties and music and devote myself to being a soldier,' he said as he broke his violin in half and put it on the fire. He never played again.

Arthur's prospects brightened when his brother bought him command of an Irish regiment.

His ill-kempt troops and dandified officers soon nicknamed him 'Nosey' on account of his large nose and his habit of enquiring into their laziness and dishonesty. Now that war had broken out with revolutionary France, 'Nosey' wanted to lead an efficient and well-trained regiment against the enemy.

His chance came when the 33rd was sent to the Low Countries. Unfortunately, the campaign was no more than a continuous retreat across icy plains and Wellesley could only try to preserve his shivering troops.

'I am so disgusted with my senior commanders that I shall leave the Army,' he angrily told his brother.

But before he could do so, the regiment was posted to India and in 1797 the Colonel landed at Calcutta to find that India was suffering from famine, banditry and ceaseless wars between rival princes. One of the most powerful rulers was Tippoo Sahib, Sultan of Mysore, who hated the British and was offering to assist the French.

In hard fighting through jungles and across rocky plains, Wellesley defeated Tippoo, stormed his capital and became the real ruler of Mysore. He put down the robber-chieftains and had established order when his borders were threatened by a vast army of the warlike Mahrattas.

By now Wellesley had learnt that the art of making war in a huge parched country lay in organizing supplies for his soldiers:

'If I had bullocks and rice, I had men,' he said, 'and if I had men, I knew I could beat the enemy.'

In a series of battles, sieges and long slogging marches, he broke the power of the Mahrattas and returned to England as Major-General Sir Arthur Wellesley.

Presently he crossed to Dublin and married Lady Kitty who had waited ten years for her hero. He was now rich and famous and he naturally expected to be given a high command against Napoleon and the all-conquering French. But the old generals pooh-poohed his Indian victories and sent him to take charge of a mere brigade on the south coast.

Suddenly, there was news from Spain. Napoleon had put his brother on the throne and the Spaniards were up in arms. So were the Portuguese whose king had been driven into exile.

'Here is our chance to take a crack at the French!' cried Wellesley to his friend Lord Castlereagh and Sir Arthur was sent to Spain with a small army.

In the years of waiting, he had thought how to beat the French. They fought in dense columns—very well, he would meet them in a double line, having trained his men to hold their fire and to finish the work with the bayonet. The French had splendid artillery—he would post his men in trenches and behind ridges for protection. The French had the best cavalry in the world—he would form his infantry into squares to stand rock-like against the fiercest charges. French armies moved fast, living on food collected on the march but he would set up supply points and follow slowly with store-waggons, as in India.

For Spain reminded him of India. In this vast, hungry land, a small army might be beaten but a big one would certainly starve and Wellesley, the master of feeding his troops, was certain he could beat the French.

His arrival brought the enemy out of Lisbon like a swarm of angry bees and they met him at Vimiero, moving in columns of attack.

'I received them in line which they are not accustomed to,' said Sir Arthur. 'Volleys halted their columns and the bayonets broke them.'

His cavalry charged and the French were defeated. At that moment, a senior general arrived from England to take over command. He ordered a halt.

'But, Sir Harry, we must advance! In three days, we shall be in Lisbon,' cried Wellesley indignantly.

But Sir Harry was old and cautious. His delay was supported by an even more senior general who made a truce with the defeated foe and actually agreed to carry them back to France in English ships!

In disgust, Wellesley demanded to be sent home and, since the public shared his disgust, the two elderly generals were brought back to face a Court of Enquiry. Meanwhile, the French crushed the Spaniards and flooded back into Portugal.

When the Court of Enquiry praised Wellesley's conduct, the Government ordered him to resume the struggle. With only 25,000 British soldiers, his task was to clear the Peninsula of 250,000 Frenchmen who hardly knew the meaning of the word defeat.

Wellesley had to go warily. His own troops were poor, the Portuguese were brave but undisciplined and he found the Spaniards useless except as guerrilla fighters.

'But I *am* at the head of the only army in Europe that is capable and willing to fight the French,' he said. 'And I do not intend to lose my army.'

Portugal was to be his base. The Royal Navy would bring supplies; mule-trains and bullock-carts would carry them to his army in the field. He was a plain man in a plain grey coat and a low cocked hat covered with oilskin. There were no valets, cooks, musicians or actresses on his Staff. If the men had bread, meat and sixty rounds of ammunition apiece, he was content.

He drove Marshal Soult out of the north and advanced into Spain, grumbling a bit about his troops: 'They are a rabble—I am endeavouring to tame them. But,' he added cheerfully, 'the ball is now at my foot and I hope I shall have the strength to kick it.'

At Talavera, 'after two days of the hardest fighting I have ever been a party to', he beat the French and promptly retreated because his army was half-starved in that barren country and the enemy was massing four huge armies against him. Napoleon sent his best general, 'the old fox' Massena, to drive the British into the sea.

That winter, Wellesley waited for the French, drilling his redcoats and his Portuguese 'fighting cocks'. Aided by thousands of civilians, he built the Lines of Torres Vedras, a series of mounds, ditches and ravines that protected Lisbon.

'Every calf, hen and sack of corn must be brought inside my lines,' ordered Wellesley, and when Massena advanced he did so through a bare countryside. After weeks of battering, he was forced to withdraw his starving army and Wellesley followed him into Spain.

In August 1812, now Lord Wellington, he rode into Madrid. High-nosed, looking straight ahead, he took no notice of the frenzied inhabitants who strewed the road with silken shawls, cheered, wept and ran alongside to kiss his sword, his stirrups and even his horse's flanks.

But he lacked the strength to hold Madrid. In driving rain, he led his army back to Portugal and prepared for the final spring. In May 1813 his red-coats, guns, waggons and bridging-teams were ready and, as they crossed the frontier, Wellington flourished his hat and cried, 'Farewell, Portugal! I shall never see you again.' He never did.

This time he drove the enemy clean out of Spain until, having beaten them all the way, he learned in the market-place of Toulouse that Napoleon had abdicated. 'Hurrah!' he cried as he snapped his fingers. 'Europe is free!'

In March 1815 the Duke was in Vienna when a servant brought a letter to his room. It stated that Napoleon had escaped from Elba and was on his way to Paris.

As the assembly of princes and statesmen broke up in alarm and the generals scurried away to raise their armies, Wellington calmly ordered a carriage to take him to Brussels.

'It is there or thereabouts that I shall have to meet the Tyrant,' he remarked.

As he rattled along, he reflected that it was a pity that his Peninsular veterans were mostly in America or on the high seas.

'Well,' he said to himself. 'I must make do with whatever troops the Allies can scrape up. At least Blücher, that stout old Prussian, will fight like a man.'

Brussels was buzzing with rumours and alarms. Mr. Creevey, an English politician staying in the city, met the Duke in a park and asked him what he thought of

his chances. Wellington looked down his long nose at the self-important little man:

'By Heaven!' he snapped. 'I think Blücher and myself can do the thing!'

Napoleon, even more confident, defeated Blücher before he could join forces with Wellington. Then he hurled his matchless cavalry against the British and their allies at Quatre Bras. The Duke was at full-stretch to rally his unsteady troops and once, almost surrounded and ahead of his own line, he had to put his horse at a ditch lined with Highlanders.

'Lie still and keep your heads down!' he cried as his horse leapt the obstacle. Then, as cool as ever, his deep voice was heard calling out:

'92nd, don't fire until I tell you.'

When he heard of the Prussian defeat, he remarked grimly:

'Old Blücher has had a good hiding and has gone eighteen miles to the rear. We must do the same. I suppose they'll say in England that we were licked. Well, I can't help that.'

He shepherded his army back towards Brussels and took up a position along a ridge near the village of

*The Battle of Waterloo*

Waterloo. The weather was cold and wet but as one of his veterans said to a shivering recruit:

'It's nothing to what we had in Spain with old Nosey.'

It was still raining at dawn and Napoleon delayed his attack to allow the ground to dry. There was no need to hurry for he was certain of victory now that Blücher was in full retreat. He was wrong. The tough old Prussian was already urging his troops across the marshes in order to keep his promise to Wellington.

At noon the French attacked. As in Spain, Wellington waited behind the ridge, his men holding their fire until the word of command.

'The Emperor did not manoeuvre at all,' said the Duke. 'He just moved forward in the old style in columns and was driven off in the old style.'

Ahead of the line there was desperate fighting round the outposts but the Guards held out all day amid the

broken walls of a château. Farther back, the infantry formed squares and withstood thunderous cavalry charges as though they were rooted to the ground. Artillerymen blazed away and worked like demons to haul their guns back to safety. The Duke was everywhere. Astride his horse 'Copenhagen', he was scribbling orders, galloping to reform a broken line, chiding and encouraging the troops:

'There, my lads, in with you!'

'Ah, that's the way I like to see horse-artillery move!'

'Hard pounding, gentlemen. We shall have to see who can pound the longest.'

He ordered the Life Guards to charge and as the survivors rode back, he was there to meet them, his hat raised:

'Life Guards, I thank you!'

Towards the end of that awful day, the British were still holding the ridge when the Prussians were seen approaching. In a last bid for victory, Napoleon ordered the invincible Imperial Guard to break the British line.

To the tap of the drum, they advanced up the slope, 6000 of them in perfect order, Marshal Ney and their officers walking in front with drawn swords. At sixty paces, a deep voice called:

'Now, Maitland. Now's your time!'

The British stood up and crashed out their terrible volley. As the smoke cleared and the Imperial Guard was seen to waver, a figure on a chestnut horse pointed with a cocked hat. The line sprang forward.

That night the vengeful Prussians kept up the

pursuit, but back at Waterloo Wellington waited at his headquarters, watching the door for the men who would not come back. In the morning, they brought him the lists of the dead and the Iron Duke wept.

He returned grim-faced to Brussels where busy Mr. Creevey came to ask him how the battle went.

'It has been a dam' serious business,' he replied. 'Blücher and I have lost 30,000 men. It was the nearest run thing you ever saw in your life.'

He walked up and down, praising the courage of his men, courage that astonished even him.

'Yes, a close-run thing,' he said, adding almost to himself. 'By Heaven! I don't think it would have done if I had not been there!'

## ELIZABETH GARRETT ANDERSON

Even before *Lucy* had nosed alongside the rickety timbers of Slaughden Quay, Mr. Garrett was bawling orders to the men ashore.

'Harry, bring the cart nearer! Lambert, don't drive forward. Back the mare, you fool! Albert, you come aboard for the boxes!'

A landing-plank was heaved into place. Boxes, chairs, tables and trunks were trundled on to the quay and hoisted into the waiting carts. Having seen to everything, Mr. Garrett turned jovially to his wife and two little girls who were clutching their mother's skirts in a fever of excitement.

'Now, my dear,' he boomed. 'You take Louie's hand and I'll have Lizzie. Upsadaisy, my pigeon.'

With Lizzie on his shoulder, he handed Mrs. Garrett ashore and soon they were rattling along the High Street to their new home on Church Hill.

It was 1840 and the Garretts had come from London to settle at Aldeburgh on the Suffolk coast. The town consisted of three rows of forlorn cottages straggling for half a mile between the shingle beach and the marshes. There were no industries, apart from fishing, and it seemed a strange place for an energetic young man to choose to set up in business.

However, within a few years, Newson Garrett had

made a comfortable fortune and for his growing family —there were to be ten children altogether—he built himself the biggest house in the town.

The Garrett children loved Aldeburgh. All summer, they swam, picnicked and ran wild. Led by Lizzie, they explored the marshes, fished, sailed and rode their ponies across the windy heathlands.

In all their games they had the boisterous support of their father. Newson Garrett was a character. He quarrelled with the parson, the town councillors and his own workmen; he had a voice like a bull and a heart as soft as butter. Everyone knew that the master's bark was worse than his bite and his children adored him but, like their father, they stood in awe of their pretty mother.

Mrs. Garrett was absolute mistress of Alde House and when she remarked one day:

'Newson, it's time those girls had a governess,' Mr. Garrett did not argue. Within a week, Miss Edgeworth arrived from London.

Poor Miss Edgeworth, in her shabby bonnet, was a typical Victorian governess. Prim and ill-educated, her one aim was to please her employer, but she had no idea how to teach lively children like the Garretts.

She owned three books—Mangnall's *Questions*, Slater's *Book of Dates* and a volume of French verbs. These and a set of rules for 'ladylike behaviour' were her sole equipment for teaching. Mornings in the schoolroom were torture but the afternoon walks were worse. Miss Edgeworth did not let up for one minute:

'No talking, if you please! Elizabeth, hold up your head! Milly, do not lag behind and put down that flower at once! Louie, repeat to me your list of verbs.'

There was no escape from 'the enemy' until the older girls discovered a way to confuse Miss Edgeworth. Secretly, they studied her horrid books until they knew them better than she did and then they would trap her with difficult questions. 'Oo, Miss

Edgeworth, yesterday you said the opposite to that,' they would shrill gleefully.

Mrs. Garrett was distressed by their naughtiness.

'I am afraid that Miss Edgeworth cannot manage our girls,' she sighed.

'The woman's a fool!' snorted Mr. Garrett. 'Better send 'em away to school.'

At Blackheath, in south London, there was a genteel finishing school for young ladies run by the two Miss Brownings. After their experience of a governess, Lizzie and Louie loved it. They made many friends and they liked the gentle Miss Brownings with their passion for fresh air and French conversation. After two years, the girls were considered 'finished' and they came home to Aldeburgh.

In Victorian days, young ladies helped to teach their small brothers and sisters, visited the poor and attended tea-parties until they married. At twenty-two, Louie married the brother of a school friend and went away to live in London but Elizabeth showed no sign of following her sister's example.

One day, she went into her father's study and said, 'Father, Jane and Annie Crowe have written to ask if I may pay them a visit.'

'So you shall, my dear. Your mother can spare you, now that Alice manages the little ones so nicely.'

'And, Father, while I am away, I want to think what I shall do with my life.'

Mr. Garrett was puzzled. Girls got married. Why should Lizzie think about anything else? With her fine eyes and determined chin, she was his favourite daughter. Didn't Mother say, 'Dear Lizzie takes after Father'?

'Are you not happy at home?' he asked gently.

'Oh yes, but I want to *do* something, to use the mind that God gave me.'

During her holiday, Elizabeth met Emily Davies, the vicar's daughter, a fiery little person with some very strange ideas about the position of women.

'What are we fitted for in life?' she demanded. 'For marriage and nothing else! Men make us into the dear dull creatures they admire. They won't let us use our brains!'

Elizabeth and Emily became close friends. They talked about things that would have shocked Mrs. Garrett and wrote long letters about their hopes of having a career. In London, they stayed with Louie and were thrilled to meet some ladies who talked about jobs for women. They went to hear a lady from America who had actually qualified as a doctor.

When Elizabeth heard this slight pale woman say, 'I never thought about failure,' she vowed that she too would never admit defeat. After the lecture, Elizabeth was introduced to the speaker who looked at her keenly and said:

'I noticed you in the audience. You have more strength than I had and I know you will succeed as a doctor.'

A woman doctor! The idea was absurd in England. 'I felt,' said Elizabeth, 'as if I were thrust into something too big for me.' But, as the weeks passed, the idea would not leave her.

She wrote to Emily. They discussed the difficulties —examinations, Latin, chemistry and other subjects that girls were never taught. And she would have to tell her parents. It was not too difficult to speak to

Father but to tell Mother was another matter.

Mrs. Garrett was horrified. She retired to her room and made herself ill with weeping. Lizzie set her obstinate mouth and went to the local schoolmaster for Latin lessons.

Mr. Garrett was too fond of his daughter to let her battle alone. In June 1860, the two of them went to London to call upon the leading doctors for advice.

'Women would make bad doctors,' said a famous surgeon coldly. 'Moreover, it would be extremely improper for them to work alongside gentlemen-students. I bid you Good-day, ma'am.'

As the day wore on, Mr. Garrett's fatherly pride was wounded by these sneering fellows in frock-coats and in the cab on the way to Louie's, he burst out:

'Drat me, Lizzie, if we don't beat the pack of them!'

From that day, it was his struggle as well as Elizabeth's and he never failed to support her with money and encouragement. Through friends, he arranged an introduction to Mr. Hawes who was on the Board of the Middlesex Hospital.

'I do not think that a young lady will be able to stand the sights and smells of a hospital ward,' said Mr. Hawes earnestly. 'But you seem determined to try so I can arrange for you to spend six months as a nurse.'

Armed with a linen apron and notebook, Elizabeth presented herself to the Matron and was taken to meet the nurses. Believing her to be a rich lady with an interest in the sick, they offered to cook for her and to do her laundry during her stay.

'No, thank you,' smiled Elizabeth. 'I would like to do all the work of a nurse, just as it is.'

Mr. Nunn, Dean of the Medical School, Dr. Willis, the senior surgeon, and Mr. Plaskitt, the apothecary, were charming and polite. Like the nurses, they had no idea what was in Elizabeth's mind.

Presently, she followed her new friends into the surgical ward. A sickening smell unnerved her for a moment but she went forward to look at the festering stump of a leg amputated below the knee.

At this time, very little was known about germs and a surgeon would put on his oldest and filthiest frock-coat for an operation and would wash his hands after but not before an amputation. As a result, surgery was desperately risky and many patients were certain to die from simple operations.

But, after the first shocks, Elizabeth found the work fascinating. Soon, she was writing to Emily:

'I begin my day by preparing lint, lotion, poultices, bandages and various ointments. While I am doing this, the sister goes round examining all the wounds. The simpler cases she now leaves to me entirely. The doctors are uncommonly civil to me . . .'

They remained civil until their visitor applied to become a medical student.

'My dear young lady, how on earth can I admit you as a student?' said the College Treasurer with amused contempt.

'By allowing me to pay the usual fees,' replied Elizabeth.

'You may certainly make a donation to the Hospital and continue as an observer, but a student, oh dear me no!'

Elizabeth said no more but, one morning, she slipped into the chemistry laboratory with the men-students. Apart from a few whistles and raised eyebrows, they said nothing and if the lecturer saw her, he gave no sign.

Emboldened by this success, Elizabeth asked the Dean if she could enter the dissecting-room.

'Well, I suppose we might give it a trial,' mused Mr. Nunn.

Elizabeth could have kissed him. She felt that she was now accepted as a real student and she worked so hard that she gained honours in every class examination.

'I beg you to keep your marks a secret,' warned one of the examiners but when a physician asked a difficult question that reduced the class to silence, Elizabeth could not help blurting out the correct answer.

Next day, her friend Mr. Plaskitt took her aside: 'Miss Garrett, I implore you not to go into lectures today. The students have signed a petition to have you dismissed.'

'But why? What harm have I done them?'

'None, but they say they are being made to look silly by a lady who has no right to be here. The College is considering the matter this morning.'

At lunchtime, Elizabeth's friends avoided her. The Dean and even Mr. Plaskitt were absent but she spied Dr. Thompson, a kindly physician. He would tell her what the Council had decided.

The doctor looked upset. He coughed and took out his watch as if in a hurry.

'My dear young lady,' he mumbled. 'Most distressing affair . . . presence of female students considered unsuitable . . . great regret . . .'

He pressed her hand, gave her a little pat of sympathy and hurried away. Elizabeth understood his meaning. After a year, the most exciting year of her life, she must go, and with her head held high to keep back the tears, she walked out of the Hospital.

At Alde House, there were thirteen cousins staying for the holidays so, between picnics and parties, it was as much as Elizabeth could do to slip away to an attic with her books. At all costs, she must keep up her studies in the hope that a college somewhere would accept her.

She wrote letter after letter and the replies were always the same. Oxford, Cambridge, London, Edinburgh, Glasgow and Dundee universities all refused to admit a woman student. The College of Surgeons would not even allow her to take its diploma for midwifery.

Fuming with indignation, Mr. Garrett took a hand. He and Elizabeth discovered that the Society of Apothecaries was bound to examine anyone who completed a five years' apprenticeship:

'Right,' cried Mr. Garrett, 'we'll creep through that loophole, Lizzie, my love.'

When Mr. Plaskitt agreed to accept Elizabeth as his 'apprentice', it seemed certain that she would qualify as a doctor but it was not what she really wanted.

'A medical degree, even a foreign one, would win more respect than an apothecary's licence,' she said.

There was just a chance that St. Andrews University might accept her, so she travelled to Scotland, where 'a dear old buffer actually wrote my name in the register and gave me a card with the magic words STUDENT OF ST. ANDREWS UNIVERSITY beneath my name'.

Alas, the authorities demanded the card back and she had to take private lessons both in Scotland and in London.

'What I need most of all is surgical knowledge,' she lamented. 'There are no dissecting-rooms open to me and Dr. H. has written me the rudest letter when I asked him for lessons in anatomy.'

'I will pay for you to study in America,' replied her father.

'No,' she answered. 'For the sake of women in England, I must qualify in England, just to prove that it can be done.'

Her obstinacy was rewarded for, in 1864, she won permission to visit the London Hospital where she

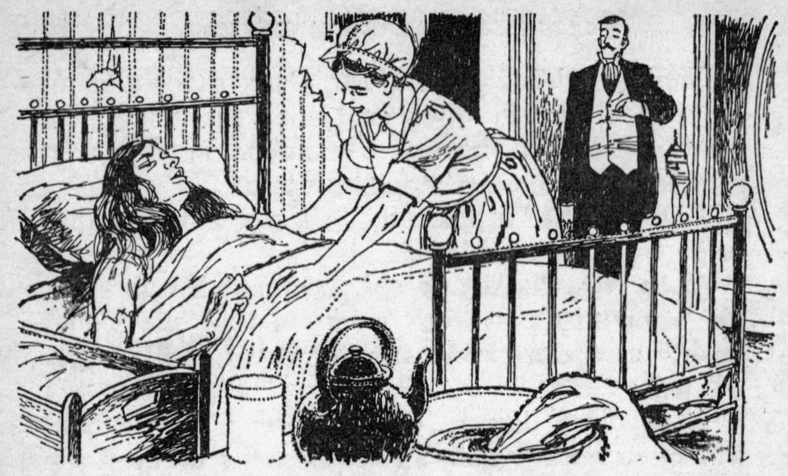

gained her first experience of midwifery in the slums of Stepney.

'I worked all night on a difficult case,' she told Emily, 'and my kind doctor allowed me to carry out the operation. He let me do everything apart from giving the chloroform. It wasn't easy but I enjoyed it immensely.'

By autumn, she had completed the course for the Society of Apothecaries and she applied to take the examination.

Forgetting their own rules, the examiners refused to accept a woman candidate but they had Mr. Garrett to deal with.

'I will sue you in every Court in the kingdom!' he thundered and the Society yielded. Elizabeth passed so high that the examiners declared it was a mercy they did not have to publish the list in order of merit for, in that case, they must have given first place to Miss Garrett.

She had done it! At long, long last, she was a doctor, the first woman to qualify in England.

As proud and happy as if he himself had qualified, Mr. Garrett took a house for Elizabeth in Upper Berkeley Street, London.

'We must put your name on the door, Lizzie,' he said. 'I have ordered a brass-plate with "Doctor Garrett" on it.'

'Oh, Father, do you not think that the title will put some strangers off. I want poor people, especially women, to know that a woman doctor lives here.'

'Then "Miss Garrett" will do very well.'

'That sounds like a dress-maker. Let us put, quite simply, "Elizabeth Garrett, L.S.A." '

## ROBERT BADEN-POWELL

He was a boy of medium-size, with freckles and red curly hair. At thirteen, he was not very good at games or lessons and his school-mates regarded Baden-Powell as an amusing card who could draw funny pictures with either hand and make them laugh with his comic songs and imitations.

Unknown to most of them, B-P had invented a secret game. Near the school was a stretch of woodland known as The Copse. It was out-of-bounds but this did not prevent B-P and two or three of his closest friends from going there on half-holidays. Years later, he confessed:

'In the Copse, I learned to snare rabbits and to cook them over the tiny fire of the bushman. I learned to use an axe and to move through the bush. I knew how to hide my tracks, to climb a tree and "freeze" there while the authorities passed below.'

Holidays were even more exciting than school for, besides enjoying tramping expeditions in Wales, Robert was cabin-boy aboard his brother's 5-ton yacht when they sailed her round Scotland to Norway.

At nineteen he had not made up his mind about a career. Half-heartedly, he sat for an Army examination, and to everyone's surprise he passed so high that he was excused the usual officer-training at Sandhurst. Instead, he was gazetted a sub-lieutenant in the 13th Hussars stationed in India.

In the eighteen-seventies, most officers were wealthy young men who enjoyed sport and the gay life of British India with little thought for the soldiers in the ranks. B-P however had to live on his pay and he showed an unusual enthusiasm for soldiering and for looking after his men. At camp concerts he became enormously popular as a comic turn, though some of officers looked down their noses at his foolery.

Some years later, a young officer named Churchill was laughing loudly at a brilliantly funny performance in a regimental concert:

'That's Baden-Powell,' whispered his companion. 'An amazing chap. Has seen no end of active service, is a marvellous polo player and is a coming man. But fancy a senior officer kicking up his legs on the stage like that!'

Along the North-West Frontier the army was constantly in action against the fierce tribesmen, and in this barren mountainous land it was dangerous to move troops without knowledge of the enemy's whereabouts. Young Baden-Powell made a name for his ability to scout ahead of the main force with small patrols that he trained himself. He taught them the skills he had begun to learn in The Copse—how to move silently, to observe the tiniest evidence of enemy movement, to remember landmarks and patches of cover.

He had been promoted Captain when the regiment returned to England for a spell of home duty. This was too quiet for B-P and he obtained permission to go to

Russia with his younger brother, an officer in the Scots Guards.

In order to find out about some secret searchlights and observation-balloons, the brothers each bought a Russian civilian hat and coolly walked into a fort and examined the equipment as though they were Russian military experts. With similar impudence, they were watching some important manoeuvres when B-P was arrested as a spy. However, he managed to warn his brother and, on the way to prison, he gave his guards the slip and escaped to a ship that carried him safely home.

After another Secret Service trip, B-P was sent to

South Africa where the Zulus had rebelled against the rule of white men. It was during this campaign that he first heard the Een-Gonyama chorus that he was later to introduce to the Boy Scouts. In honour of their chief, the Zulu warriors chanted:

> 'Een-Gonyama! Gonyama! Invooboo!
> Yabo! Yabo! Invooboo!'

meaning:

> 'He is a lion, a lion! He is a hippopotamus!
> Yes, sir! Yes, sir! He is a hippopotamus!'

During the Ashanti campaign in West Africa, B-P commanded native troops whose duty was to scout ahead of the army through dense jungle criss-crossed by swift streams. For this work he found it best to divide the men into small companies, each under a patrol-leader. He himself took to wearing a wide-brimmed 'cowboy' hat to protect his face from low branches and, in the open, from the fierce African sun. He also found it useful to carry a long pole marked in feet and inches for this helped him to cross streams, to test swampy ground and to make quick measurements.

For his good work in West Africa, B-P was promoted Lieutenant-Colonel and, soon afterwards, he took part in the Matabele War, 'my best adventure', as he called it.

In wild, hilly country, small British forces were trying to subdue a brave wily enemy and it was B-P's job to track down the tribesmen and discover their strongholds. By day he organized operations and at night he went out alone or with a single companion into the Matoppo Hills.

A war correspondent wrote this about him:

'Wearing soft rubber-soled shoes, B-P used to spend nights prowling about, spying on the rebels, calculating their numbers and locating their camping-grounds. One night he took me with him. Walking with an easy swing, he stepped into the darkness amidst the giant boulders of the Matoppos where he seemed completely at home. He led me by a rough path on to a kop. Peering over, we could see, not 500 yards away, the fires of an impi (native force). Signing me to be silent, we watched for a few minutes and presently moved off by another path. "Never return by the same road," he whispered. It was with a sigh of relief that I found myself back in camp. I never asked to be taken again.'

The Matabele warriors gained so great a respect for the Colonel who harried them that they named him 'Impeesa'—'the wolf that never sleeps'.

In 1899 B-P was sent to Rhodesia with orders to train two mounted regiments and he had just taken up his headquarters in the town of Mafeking when the Boers declared war on Britain.

Mafeking, an outpost town in the veldt, contained stores of food and railway equipment but it had no defences. B-P immediately set to work to build a 7-mile ring of forts and earthworks connected to his H.Q. by trenches and telephone lines. Wells were dug and shelters prepared for the civilian population since the town contained about 250 white persons and 8000 natives of the Baralong tribe.

To hold this outpost B-P had only 1250 soldiers and no artillery apart from seven small guns that were old and almost useless. However, his slender force had manned the forts and the Colonel was up in his look-out post when the Boer army was seen approaching.

General Cronje surrounded Mafeking with 10,000 men and began a bombardment. After several hours, he sent a messenger under flag of truce demanding surrender 'to prevent further bloodshed'.

'What bloodshed?' enquired B-P. 'Tell your general that I shall be obliged to know when it starts. So far, the only blood shed has been one chicken's!'

During the siege that followed, B-P kept up the townsfolk's spirits by posting up copies of his impudent replies to the Boer commander. He started a newspaper, the *Mafeking Mail*, that was issued daily, 'shells permitting', and he devised all kinds of tricks to deceive the enemy.

Bogus orders were blared through camp megaphones, dummy figures were placed in the forts and false information was allowed to fall into the hands of spies inside the town. To discourage night-attacks, B-P pretended that he was well supplied with searchlights—actually he had only one, made out of a biscuit-tin nailed to a pole, but at night it was rushed round from one fort to another, giving out a few flashes at each to make it seem as if a whole series of searchlights was being tested.

Not content merely to sit still and await relief, B-P soon went on the attack and pushed back the Boer lines by night charges and by using a train that puffed up and down, its crew firing at the enemy until the lines were destroyed. The lack of artillery was partly

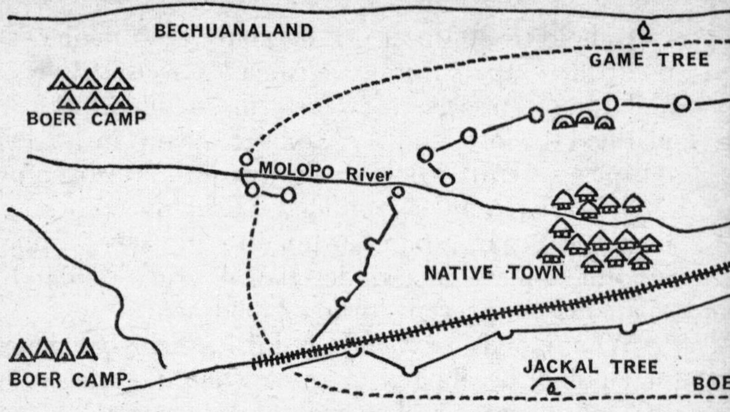


overcome when the railwaymen made a howitzer called 'The Wolf' out of a steam-pipe reinforced with iron railings and they provided iron cannon-balls for an old 18th-century gun-barrel that someone discovered was being used as a gate-post!

'It was all a game of bluff from start to finish,' said B-P but as the weeks turned into months he knew that the position was serious. To keep boredom at bay, he organized games, competitions, concerts and even a baby-show but the greatest worry was food. Horses, dogs and mules were killed to eke out the rations. Nothing was wasted and when the skins and bones had been boiled for brawn and soup, even the manes and tails were used to stuff mattresses in the hospital.

Fifty men were killed in an attack on a Boer post at Game Tree Hill and, from then on, the garrison had to stay on the defensive and endure the shelling.

After seven months, news began to filter into the town that the British were advancing. At this, the

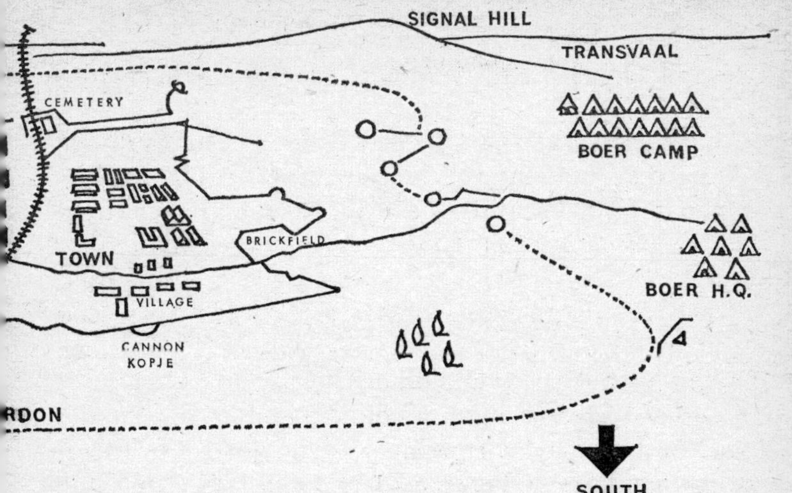


Boers redoubled their efforts and they succeeded in breaking in at one point until B-P, watching from his tower, regrouped his forces and drove them out.

At last the Boers could be seen withdrawing and from distant hills General Plumer flashed a message, 'How are you getting on?' B-P replied in one word, 'Welcome!'

At seven that evening, the British force entered Mafeking. The siege was over. 'We all tried to speak at once,' said an engineer. 'But we could only gaze at each other and say senseless things like "By Jove!" and "Well, I'm hanged!" One man tried to cheer, buried his face in his hands and sobbed. It had been 217 days.'

The joy of the Mafeking garrison was nothing compared with the outburst in Britain. On 'Mafeking Night', people went mad, lit bonfires and danced in the streets. Baden-Powell was a public hero.

His picture was everywhere, the Queen sent her personal congratulations and he was promoted to the rank of General, the youngest general in the British Army.

It was several years before B-P reached England, where he found himself famous, not only because of Mafeking but because of a little book he had written called *Aids to Scouting*. In it, to help young soldiers, he had described what he had learned in India and Africa about tracking, observation, map-work and even spying.

The book turned out to be a best-seller. Thousands of copies were supplied to soldiers embarking for the war and, more surprisingly, schoolmasters, Boys' Brigade officers and club leaders bought it because the book was full of ideas that appealed to boys.

B-P found so much enthusiasm for the kind of woodcraft and outdoor activities that he described, that he decided to hold an experimental camp. Twenty boys were invited to Brownsea Island where they were divided into four 'patrols' called Wolves, Curlews, Bulls and Ravens. There was no uniform but each was asked to bring 'shorts', a most unusual garment in those days.

Each morning, the camp was roused at 6 a.m. by a Koodoo horn that B-P had captured in Africa and the day was given over to tracking, stalking, life-saving and boating. The boys also had the usual chores of camping. There were games, night patrols and expeditions to allow the boys to cook and fend for themselves and the day usually ended with camp-fire yarns and the Een-Gonyama chorus.

This camp at Brownsea Island was the start of the Boy Scout Movement. Having seen the boys' terrific enthusiasm, B-P re-wrote his soldiers' handbook and

called it *Scouting for Boys*. In 1908 the book appeared in fortnightly parts and almost at once thousands of boys began to form their own scout troops.

Within a year B-P was faced with the problem of 60,000 scouts with no rules, uniforms or leaders. He never meant this to happen.

'I did not intend to have a separate organization of Boy Scouts,' he said. 'I hoped the Boys' Brigade and the Y.M.C.A. would use the idea. But the movement grew up of itself.'

Some alarming stories reached him. One boy read the book and went off and organized a gang of his own. They set fire to some property while trying to light a camp-fire, got marooned on top of a church tower and, having been rescued, put out to sea on a home-made raft and were brought back by life-boat! Enthusiastic youngsters like these clearly needed B-P's help. But he was a senior Army officer. Should he not devote himself to his real career rather than to a boys' movement that might fizzle out as quickly as it had begun?

The War Office solved his problem by suddenly placing him on the retired list. It is still a mystery why this able soldier was put on one side at the age of fifty but, as Sir Winston Churchill said, 'How lucky for him and how lucky for us all.'

At once B-P threw himself heart and soul into the new work. He toured the country, explaining the idea of Scouting, appealing for funds and help from anyone who was interested. He was a humorous speaker with dozens of stories from his adventures and the public soon realized that a new Movement had arrived. What kind of movement was it?

Some people expected that a retired General would turn boys into little soldiers. They wanted drill and Army discipline. Others felt that scouting ought to be linked to their Church. Some wanted B-P to forbid drink, smoking, Sunday games or some other pet dislike.

B-P was firm with these well-meaning people.

'Scouting is merely a step to help develop a boy into a capable and happy man,' he said. 'Scouting is fun.'

He wanted as few rules as possible, merely a simple law or promise so that boys of every kind and religion could come in. Friendly with everyone, he still followed his own ideals. The Scout Headquarters was set up to train scoutmasters and to obtain funds and camping-sites. There was a weekly magazine in which B-P wrote articles illustrated by his own comical sketches and he devised a uniform based upon what his men wore in the South African Constabulary—the wide-brimmed hat, the shorts and tough shirt, the scarf that could be used as a sling or bandage and the staff marked in feet and inches.

When a system of badges was started, B-P fought hard to prevent badges becoming another kind of examination:

'Scouting is a GAME!' he cried. 'If a boy is a *trier*, no matter how clumsy, his examiner can award him the badge and this will inspire him to go on trying.'

As early as 1909 the scouts made their first big public appearance when 10,000 Boy Scouts gathered at the Crystal Palace. B-P was going round to see various activities when he came across a small band of girls wearing scout hats and scarves. He stopped, looked them up and down and his eyes twinkled as he asked who they were.

'Please, we are Girl Scouts and we want to do scouting like the boys.'

Thus the Girl Guide Movement came into being. Wolf Cubs, Brownies, Sea Scouts and Rovers were founded for the same reason—simply because boys and girls wanted to take part in the movement that B-P had started.

He devoted the rest of his life to scouting, travelling all over the world to encourage new associations that were springing up. Always he was lecturing, writing and sketching because his books and articles paid for his journeys and did not cost the scout movement a penny. Yet he never seemed to be harassed or overworked. Scouting was fun and the Chief Scout enjoyed it all.

There were huge Jamborees when thousands of Scouts from dozens of nations travelled to London, Denmark, Australia, Hungary and Holland. On these occasions, no man was more hero-worshipped than B-P but he remained as humorous and modest as ever. Over and over again, scouts found themselves chatting to a friendly scoutmaster who asked them questions, teased them a bit and got them to talk about their homes and interests. Only later did they discover that he was Chief Scout of the world.

At Pax Hill in Hampshire scouts were always welcome to camp in his grounds and if they woke early enough, they might see the Chief (who slept out of doors winter and summer) up and about at five o'clock, walking with his dogs, gardening or writing some of those innumerable letters and articles before most people had breakfasted. But he had time to joke with the smallest scout and to put him at ease—'A scout is a brother to every other scout,' he would say.

He was over eighty when he went to South Africa to see how the scouts were faring in the country he loved. His health failed and he settled in Kenya where he continued to write and to draw the wild animals that came almost to his door.

B-P died there in 1941 and among his papers were found messages to Boy Scouts and Girl Guides. The last words he wrote were these:

'The most worthwhile thing is to try and put a bit of happiness into the lives of others.'

# LORD NUFFIELD

The bicycle stood ready. It had been mended and was almost as good as new.

'How much, boy?' asked the undergraduate.

'Front fork straightened, new spokes, brake blocks—four shillings,' replied the boy. He took the money, wrote the amount in a small notebook and turned to get on with another repair job.

William Richard Morris was fifteen, a wiry little chap with a thatch of dark hair and a determined jaw. As he worked he was adding up in his mind the value of the repairs he had done that week. Already it came to several times the five-shillings wage that he would receive on Saturday.

Presently, the boy's employer came into the shop.

'If you please, I wish to ask for a rise of a shilling a week,' said William abruptly.

'Five shillings is a very good wage, Morris, and it's all you'll get from me!'

William wiped his hands on a piece of rag and took his cap from a nail.

'It's all you'll ever pay me,' he said. 'Good morning.'

When he reached his home in James Street, Oxford, William's mother was alarmed to learn that her son had given himself the sack.

'What will you do now? Whom will you work for?' she asked.

'I have decided that no-one will pay me such good wages as W. R. Morris, so I am going to work for him!' he replied loftily.

William's father was a mild, easy-going man who had never earned much money and, when he came home for dinner, he raised no objection to his son's plan.

'Why not start in our garden shed?' he said. 'It only wants sweeping out but we'll have to buy a bench and a few tools.'

Thus, in 1892, Will Morris set up in business as a cycle repairer. Nearly everyone in Oxford went to work or to college by bicycle and there were plenty of repairs for a willing lad who would work until midnight to get a job finished.

One day Mr. Pilcher, the rector, called in at James Street. He was a very tall man and he needed an exceptionally large bicycle. Could William make one for him?

Young Morris made up a bicycle with a 27-inch frame to which he added 28-inch wheels and best-quality fittings. Mr. Pilcher was delighted and there could have been no better advertisement than the sight of the rector's outsize bicycle in the streets of Oxford.

Having made one machine, William began to make others and it was not long before he was using his mother's front parlour as a showroom. Larger premises were needed so he decided to rent a shop in the High Street and to advertise himself as:

'W. R. Morris, Practical Cycle Maker and Repairer. Sole maker of the celebrated Morris cycles.'

In order to prove his bicycles, Morris took up cycle-racing with the same determination as he did everything else. Having made a light-weight machine, he started training late at night, and since he was strong and had no thought of being anywhere but first, he soon won several cups and medals. By 1900 he was champion of three counties and had held the one-mile and the fifteen-mile championship cups for two years. One more win would make the cups his own property but, for some reason, the races were not held for a couple of seasons. Then a letter arrived asking for the return of the cups since the organizers assumed that Morris had retired from racing.

'That's where they're wrong,' snorted W. R. 'Alfred, get my racer out, I'm starting training tonight. Those cups are not leaving our shop window!'

There was only a fortnight and his shoulders and leg-muscles ached abominably for the first few days but he trained hard and in the mile race, he got away fast to discourage the others. Only one rider was able to keep with him but, with 400 yards to go, he was almost exhausted.

'I was desperately tired,' he said, 'but I thought to myself that the other fellow must be tired too. It was a question of who could hang on longest and I did.'

He won by a length and, in the fifteen-mile race, he again set such a pace that the rest of the field dropped out and he finished alone. Morris kept the cups.

Business was so good that a disused stable had to be rented as a workshop and the staff of W. R. Morris, Cycle Maker, grew to five men and two boys, one of them Alfred Keen, a tiny little chap, a brilliant mechanic, who stayed with the 'Boss' for fifty years. Like the rest of the staff, Alfred wore a white jersey embroidered back and front with the words:

'Ride Morris Cycles.'

Bicycles brought in good money but it was the new motor-cars that really interested W. R. and whenever a car broke down in the High Street, he was quickly on the spot. Engines fascinated him and he missed no opportunity to find out how they worked and why they went wrong.

'I never had a lesson on an engine,' he boasted, 'but once I saw a thing done, I could do it myself.'

After various experiments, Morris fitted a $2\frac{3}{4}$-h.p. de Dion engine to one of his cycle frames. The frame was specially strengthened and the driving-chain was enclosed in a metal casing in order to keep out dirt and rain.

'Alfred, we'll build two models for the Cycle Show,' he cried triumphantly.

The parts were ordered but, with only a few days to go, they had not arrived. Morris took off his jacket:

'I'll have to make them myself,' he said.

For four days and nights, he worked without stopping, except for an occasional nap in a chair. When the machines were finished, he decided to take them himself to London and he arrived at the Exhibition Hall just in time to put his cycles on their stand. Presently he was taking orders for the first Morris

motor-vehicle and this success enabled him to open a garage for motor-car repairs.

One day a wealthy undergraduate walked in and asked to speak to him. He and a friend were keen to go into the motor-business if they could find a partner with the necessary knowledge of engines. Would he care to join them?

Thus, *The Oxford Automobile and Cycle Agency* was born. Workshops and a showroom were opened but while Morris worked day and night, his partners spent money like water. Not surprisingly, the business collapsed, and in 1904 Morris had nothing left but his own kit of tools.

'I'll have to start again from the floor,' he said grimly. 'And I've learnt one or two things. Never spend an unnecessary penny. Put every ha'penny into production and never trust those educated college gentlemen!'

He went back to the shed in James Street. It was a hard year, for he now had a young wife to support, but his name was good and he still made the best bicycles in Oxford.

By now all kinds of motor-cars were coming on to the road and most of them gave trouble. Morris carried out repairs and, one night, working late, he said to his wife when she came to call him for supper:

'Look at this thing! Much too complicated and expensive. What people want is a reliable car at a reasonable price and I'm going to make it for them!'

Meanwhile, he drove round the country, demonstrating new cars, testing and delivering them. It was lowly work for a man with big ideas but as soon as he reached home, his spirits rose. He would hurry to his workshop for there, at the far end, was the car that he was building. Canvas hood, wooden running-board, brass-rimmed headlamps and bull-nosed radiator had been assembled by his own hands and because he made it in his own city, he called it the Morris-Oxford.

The new car appeared in the 1912 Motor Show and was praised by the experts. It was 'a two-seated flush torpedo, painted pearl-grey, upholstered in leather and brass-mounted'. Under the snub-nosed bonnet was a 10-h.p. water-cooled engine and the car 'complete and ready for the road' was priced at £175.

Several dealers ordered the new Morris-Oxford, so William found a backer and moved to a disused school next to Cowley Church. The main schoolroom became the assembly space and above, in a loft, was the paintshop staffed by Bill Anstey and a boy. William's father became clerk to the firm that numbered twelve workers including the Boss. He himself took the headmaster's study for his office where he placed above the mantel-piece a glass-case containing his cycling medals.

On the school-room floor were laid out the parts for each car—chassis, axle, transmission-set, engine, gear-box, etc. While the parts were hammered and bolted together, Bill Anstey and the boy painted the wheels grey or blue and let them down on a rope from the loft. The wheels were fitted, a box was tied on the chassis and a lad named George Lucas jumped on and drove the car out of the works, up a hill and back again. Having been tested, it was ready for the finishing touches—body, mudguard, hood, lamps.

Sometimes the works turned out as many as thirty cars in a week and still the orders came in for more. Morris, known as 'Uncle' to the men, was salesman, buyer, engineer, designer and inspector. His pale blue eyes were as sharp as gimlets and his tongue was merciless to anyone who scamped a job. He drove the men hard but he filled them with his own enthusiasm whether it was for work or for football.

The greatest problem was to find suppliers who could deliver the parts that Morris needed, for the British motor-trade was not used to being hustled. A Birmingham manufacturer once telephoned White and Poppe who made the Morris-Oxford engines.

'Mr. Poppe, there's a crazy young fellow here from Oxford. His name is Morris and he wants us to supply him with 3000 transmission-sets. Is he all right? Has he got the money?'

Mr. Poppe answered briefly:

'Morris is all right. At least, I hope he is—I've just agreed to make him 3000 engines!'

But W. R. was never satisfied. In 1914, determined to find out how Henry Ford turned out such vast numbers of cars, he sailed to New York, taking with him a brilliant Norwegian designer named 'Pop' Landstad. In America he went to see manufacturers who could supply parts more cheaply than in England, and as he went round their factories he kept a sharp look-out for ideas that would be useful. Then he would rush back to his hotel where Landstad put the ideas on to his drawing-board.

Having placed some big orders, Morris returned to Oxford eager to bring out a bigger car called the Morris Cowley. But the Great War started.

For four years weapons were more important than cars and the Morris works turned out hand-grenades, shell-cases and special parts for sea-mines required by the Navy. A few models of the Morris Cowley were made in a corner of the factory but when the war ended there was only a small stock of parts and the American firms could supply no more.

'We can make a start with what's left of the stock,' said Morris to Landstad, 'but we must get engines from somewhere.'

In Coventry he found a firm named Hotchkiss that was short of work and he took along Landstad's drawings of the American engine.

'Can you make this for £50?' he asked.

The chief engineer looked doubtful.

'It's a very keen price,' he said, 'but we will do it.'

Thus the excellent Morris-Hotchkiss 11·9-h.p. engine came to be used in the new Morris cars. A radiator firm was in difficulties, so W. R. bought it and when the firm that supplied car-bodies could not keep

*The new assembly-line layout*

up with his orders, he bought that too. But most parts were made for him by independent firms.

'I only buy a concern when they can't produce enough for my programme,' he remarked.

The Cowley works were enlarged and laid out in a new way. Instead of the men moving about from one job to another, W. R. put them into sections that dealt with only one part—the wheels were fitted to the chassis and the car was pushed to the next section that fitted the engine and so on until the car reached the paint-shop. A man did the same job all day long and if his work was less interesting than in the old days, his pay was good and the cars rolled out in ever-increasing numbers.

Morris was still the Boss who worked longer and harder than anyone else and he collected a team of brilliant men to carry out his ideas.

'All of us worshipped the ground W. R. Morris walked on,' said Miles Thomas. 'His wish was our command. He was a lonely man for the reason that he strongly preferred to think alone.'

He inspired everyone who worked for him yet he could be strangely touchy and mean.

For years he was on bad terms with the heads of Oxford University and suspicious of anyone with a 'college education'. In the early days, a wealthy friend who had put £35,000 into his business once found Morris busy at a bench testing some carburettors.

'What are you doing?' he said jokingly. 'Why don't you leave that job to experts who understand it?' Morris's face darkened. He was proud of his engineering skill and had made a special study of carburettors. He said nothing but next day he called on his bank manager. Was his account strong enough to write a big cheque? It was? Good. He sent a cheque for £35,000 to his friend and never spoke to him again.

Yet this lonely, ruthless man would take the closest interest in a workman who was seriously ill and would have him treated at his own expense. A tramp at his door was certain of a meal and tobacco and on more than one occasion the owner of an ancient Morris-Oxford was astonished to have it completely overhauled for nothing.

After the war, business was booming for a time and then came the slump.

'People simply can't afford to buy cars,' said one of Morris's directors.

'Then we'll make 'em cheaper!' snapped W. R. 'Bring me the cost-sheets.'

He peered at every item. A pound could be saved here, ten pounds there and the company's profit could be cut to the bone.

'Tell the Press, £100 off the price of the Morris Cowley!' he said.

'The man's mad. He'll ruin himself,' cried his rivals.

'No, I won't,' grinned W. R. 'Any profit is better than a loss. At least I shall still be selling motor-cars!'

When other firms had to close down, the Morris works were going at full pressure. From 60 cars a week, production rose until one Morris car was finished every five minutes of the day and still W. R. studied the costs.

'People say I'm mean. I know they do. I'm always round the works cutting down and saving expense,' he said. 'But the one object of my life has been to make cars that people can buy.'

He lived in a small house, drove an old car and was never known to waste a penny or take a holiday. He always wore a cheap suit and one evening, early on in his career as a successful employer, he called on Dr. Girdlestone, a surgeon who had founded a hospital for crippled children in some old Army huts near Oxford. The doctor's housekeeper told him that a workman was at the door.

'What can I do for you?' enquired Girdlestone.

'I understand your hospital is very hard up.'

'That is so. We need money badly,' replied the surgeon, wondering what this had to do with his shabby caller.

'I know something of your work. Perhaps you'll accept this,' said the man holding out an envelope. When he had gone, Girdlestone opened the envelope. Inside was a cheque for £1000 signed 'W. R. Morris'. It was his first gift to a hospital.

A stream of new cars continued to leave the Cowley works—the Morris Oxford, Morris Cowley, the little Morris Minor that did 'a 100 m.p.h. and 100 miles to the gallon', the big Isis, the MG sports, the Morris Eight and various vans and lorries. In addition, there were cars produced by firms that Morris took over, such as Wolseley Motors and Rileys, and as his riches grew so did his gifts.

He always believed that he suffered from ill-health, though apart from indigestion and sleeplessness, he was as hard as nails. However, his horror of illness made him determined to do something to relieve pain and disease.

From 1927 onwards he began to make gifts to

hospitals. There was £140,000 for the Radcliffe Infirmary at Oxford, £104,000 to St. Thomas's and £70,000 to rebuild Dr. Girdlestone's hospital for children. By the thirties, he had practically adopted Guy's Hospital and he ended his long feud with Oxford University by making one enormous gift after another.

In recognition of his generosity, W. R. became Sir William Morris, Oxford gave him an honorary degree and in 1936, taking his title from a pretty village near Cowley, he became Lord Nuffield.

The gifts continued—extensions to hospitals, nurses' homes, a new church, a college for priests, help for the blind and for areas where there was bad unemployment. He sold some shares in his company for £5,000,000 in order to give it all away.

'I was getting tired of working for myself,' he said. 'I could just as easily go back to where I started. In fact, I might be happier if I did.'

He offered £1,250,000 for a Medical School at Oxford and when he learned that even this vast sum was not enough, he said quietly 'I would like to increase my donation to two million pounds.'

A year later, he gave another million to found Nuffield College and there were gifts to other universities, as well as grants for cancer research, 'iron lungs' and the development of penicillin, for Boy Scouts, the Y.W.C.A., the Red Cross and for men in the Forces.

Not everyone admired the millionaire. Some people seemed to feel enraged by the size of his fortune.

'It's an advertisement for Morris cars,' they said. 'He only gives away his money instead of paying income-tax.'

This was untrue, for Nuffield was giving away his capital, not his income. When he sold great blocks of shares, he was parting with the business that he had started in a garden-shed, but he made sure that the money was put into the hands of trustworthy persons. Begging letters went into the waste-paper basket:

'I don't give money to individuals,' he would say. 'It's too risky. Giving money away is a serious business. You have to make sure that it's going to do more good than harm.'

While the Second World War was still being fought, he made the greatest of all his gifts—ten million pounds to set up the Nuffield Foundation, a fund that was to advance the health and well-being of people of all ages. To obtain this enormous sum, he sold the last of his shares:

'I myself no longer own a single share in Morris Motors,' he announced and, to the chorus of thanks, he replied:

'I don't do it for thanks but because it needs doing.'

Gradually, he gave up control of his vast business

and settled into old age. His wife died, he had no children, so he busied himself in his workshop mending watches, tinkering with bits of machinery. In 1963 Nuffield died at the age of eighty-five.

Throughout his life, W. R. gave the impression that he was a ruthless man of business. He rarely smiled and could never play the part of the beaming, warm-hearted donor, yet all his happiness came from building up a vast fortune in order to help those in need.

'With the strong, he was very hard,' said one of his friends, 'but with the old, young and sick, he was full of compassion.'

# AMY JOHNSON

A slim fair-haired girl stood in the corridor outside the Headmistress's door. On her head she wore a white Panama hat and there were giggles as each class went by on the way to Assembly.

'Amy Johnson in trouble again,' whispered one of the girls.

'What's she done this time?'

'Ringleader of a revolt against our beastly straw hats. She persuaded all the Third Form not to wear them but they let her down and she was the only one to turn up in a Panama. She's got to stand there all day wearing the thing!'

At the Boulevard School, Hull, the staff regarded Amy as a harum-scarum rebel. She was clever but her behaviour was shocking. She played all the boys' games, was the only girl who could bowl overarm and was the most daring gymnast in the school. Often she would play truant and go off alone all day on bicycle rides with a pocketful of biscuits stolen from the larder.

There was adventure in the family, for Amy's grandfather, a Dane, had run away to sea and her father had taken part in the Klondyke goldrush of 1898 before settling down in Hull.

'Had I been a man, I might have explored the Poles or climbed Mount Everest,' said Amy. 'But, as it was, my spirit found its outlet in the air. Everything in my life has spelt adventure.'

From school, Amy went to Sheffield University, where she was gay and restless. She danced, played games, changed her 'digs' dozens of times and got so much into debt that she had to borrow £50 from a friend. By last-minute swotting, she passed her degree and decided to leave.

'I don't want to teach,' she told her parents. 'I think I shall go into business.'

After three months of trying to learn typing and shorthand, she got a job in Hull at £1 a week and hated it. Her shorthand was so bad that she could not read it back, but the secret of that £50 worried her into finding another job at thirty shillings a week. She gave her mother five shillings, kept five shillings for herself and paid off the debt at £1 a week. On the day the last pound was paid, she walked out of the office.

'What are your plans now?' enquired her father. 'Would you like me to pay your fare to Canada where Uncle Edward will find you a job?'

'No thank you, Father. I'm going to try my luck in London,' replied Amy.

With enough money from her father to last a month, she arrived in the capital to look for work. Jobs were scarce and her money was running short when, in desperation, she accepted a month's trial as an assistant on the ribbons counter of a big store. At the end of her first week, a note in her pay-envelope said, 'Your services have been valued at 4s. 7½d.'

It looked as if she would have to go back home to tell her father that she had failed again when she met an old family friend who offered her a post in his solicitor's office. Her salary would be three pounds a week.

At last she was independent and able to afford to share a flat with a girl from college. The flat was not far from Stag Lane aerodrome, and at weekends, when the girls played tennis, the sky was full of aeroplanes. They fascinated Amy.

'Often I would stop and gaze wistfully skywards,' she wrote. 'I envied those pilots. . . . I had always wanted freedom and adventure and I felt that flying could give these to me.'

One Saturday, hardly realizing where she was going, she took a bus to Stag Lane. The planes were almost overhead as they glided in to land. Breathless with excitement, she ran past a notice saying 'London Aeroplane Club: Private' and found herself on the grass of the aerodrome.

People were watching the planes landing and taking off and no-one took any notice as Amy sat herself down in a deckchair outside a club-house. For an hour, she watched enthralled. She knew what she was going to do. She *must* learn to fly.

Summoning up her courage, she spoke to an instructor:

'Excuse me, how much does it cost to learn?'

'Two pounds an hour, miss, for instruction. Thirty shillings an hour solo.'

Amy did some quick mental arithmetic. At a pinch, she could just afford it.

'Can I start now?' she asked innocently.

'Not quite, miss. You have to apply to the secretary to join the Club. I warn you, there's a waiting-list.'

It was several months before she took her first lesson and it was not a success. The flying helmet that Amy borrowed was so enormous that the earphones almost met under her chin and she could not understand a word that the instructor was saying.

'Hopeless,' he said when they came down. 'You'll never learn to fly and you're simply wasting your money and my time!'

Instead of bursting into tears, Amy set her jaw. Never learn to fly? She would show him!

Next week, she went up with a different helmet and a different instructor, who found her quick to learn and extraordinarily cool-headed.

Within a few weeks, she was ready to make her first solo flight. She taxied her little yellow plane across the grass, and waited for the take-off signal.

The De Havilland Moth gathered speed until, exactly as she had been taught, she pulled the stick gently back. She was airborne—alone!

In July 1929, after fifteen hours' instruction, Amy obtained her pilot's licence. Her greatest ambition had come true.

From now on, all her spare time was spent at Stag

Lane. Since she could not afford to fly every day, she took to nosing about in the workshops. As she watched the mechanics, she became so interested in engines that she asked if she could study for the ground engineer's licence. Mr. Humphreys the chief engineer scratched his chin and said:

'Well, I suppose there's a first time for everything, Miss Johnson. I've never heard of a woman mechanic but if you can get up early, we'll see how you go along.'

For two years Amy worked on engines from six o'clock in the morning until eight. Then she rushed to the office for her day's work and hurried back in the evening to return to the workshops. At weekends she was there all day. Armed with oil-can, grease-gun and spanner, she learned to clean petrol filters, to check plugs, to strip an engine and to re-assemble it perfectly. The men accepted her as one of themselves when they

found that she never tried to dodge the dirtiest and heaviest jobs. She had a sense of fun and a real knack with engines so they felt proud when 'Johnnie' became the first woman ever to hold a ground engineer's certificate.

'If ever anyone lives for flying, it's that girl,' declared Mr. Humphreys.

Her employers obviously thought the same, for they told her that she must choose between her hobby and her office work. Amy chose flying.

'But who will employ a woman pilot?' asked Mr. Johnson.

'If I can prove that I'm as good a pilot as a man, I'll find plenty of work. I mean to make a big flight—not as a stunt but to get the money to make flying my real career.'

'And where will you go on this "big flight"?'

Amy flicked over the pages of an atlas and put her finger-tip on the map of Australia.

'I shall go *there*,' she said.

What a mad idea! thought her father. Never would he agree to such folly but, to enable her to obtain a commercial licence, he agreed to give her £150.

Amy returned to London intent on finding someone to support her plans. A newspaper editor showed no more faith in her talk of flying to Australia than if she had said she was going to ride up Mount Everest on a bicycle. In any case, the flight had been done by a crew of four in a *Vimy* bomber and quite recently that brilliant pilot, Bert Hinkler, had reached Australia in the incredible time of 15½ days.

Flying experts advised Amy to abandon the idea. A girl who had never even flown across the Channel must be out of her mind to think of flying 12,000 miles on her own.

But Amy persevered. After calling on all kinds of important people and writing hundreds of letters, she was sent to Lord Wakefield, a most generous supporter of civil aviation.

'I admire your pluck, young lady, but isn't flying to Australia too big a task for a girl?' asked Lord Wakefield. 'Have you a plane?'

'Not yet, but I know one that is absolutely ideal,' replied Amy eagerly. 'It's Captain Hope's D.H. Moth, the one he used to photograph the Prince of Wales' route over Africa. It's not new but it already has extra fuel tanks and I am planning to put another one in the passenger-seat.'

'What's the price?'

'Six hundred pounds—a perfect bargain!'

'Hm, if you were a man, Miss Johnson, I'd give you a job as a salesman. If you can get £300 yourself, I'll put up the other half and pay for your petrol into the bargain.'

Joyfully, Amy went home and persuaded her father to give her the £300 that she needed. The plane was hers and, in gratitude to her father, she christened it *Jason* after his business trademark.

On May 5th, 1930, she was ready. *Jason*, painted green and with a spare propeller tied to its side, was taxied on to the field of Croydon Aerodrome and, having waved to her father and the two or three friends who came to see her off, Amy took off and headed away to the south-east.

As she crossed the Channel, Amy's mind went over the route she had carefully planned. First stop, Vienna, then Constantinople. After Europe had been left behind, she must use the landing-fields that the R.A.F. had set up for the route to India. The Dutch had some airfields in the East Indies and the last stage would be across the lonely Timor Sea to Port Darwin. She looked proudly along the wings of her plane. The D.H. Moth was a tiny aircraft, no longer than two parked cars, but it behaved beautifully and would cruise all day at 80 m.p.h. Normally, it carried two persons but the passenger space was filled with the extra petrol tank and Amy, wearing a parachute, was strapped into the rear seat of the open cockpit.

From time to time, she checked her position . . . Belgium . . . the Rhine . . . that big town must be Frankfurt. Late in the afternoon, she picked up the Danube and, after ten hours' flying, she landed at Aspern aerodrome, Vienna. She had covered 800 miles.

No fuss was made of the pilot who booked in for a room in the airport building and took off after breakfast. She followed the Danube across Hungary and turned south over Bulgaria to reach Constantinople after twelve long hours in the cockpit.

Her departure next morning was noted by a newspaperman who sent word to London that a girl flying a Moth G-AAAH had taken off for Aleppo, 500 miles away. This report in the evening papers caused some mild interest and, next day, readers learned that the solitary flyer was past Aleppo and still going well.

Who was she? A typist from Hull? Funny thing for a girl to do all by herself.

From Aleppo the way was across 500 miles of desert. Amy had been warned of the danger of sandstorms, but throughout the morning she was more concerned about the terrific heat that made the metal parts of her aircraft impossible to touch. Ahead she noticed a dark haze.

With terrifying suddenness a storm hit the little plane, whirling it about as though it were a leaf caught by the wind. Amy's eyes and nostrils filled with sand that almost choked her and she sensed that *Jason*'s engine was not firing properly. The plane plunged down to within a few feet of the ground and it was only by fighting with all her strength that she managed to make a landing. Jumping down, she hung on to the tail to prevent *Jason* from being blown over and smashed. During a lull, she took all her luggage out of the cockpit and piled it against the wheels as a makeshift anchor.

As the wind slackened, rather than risk a night in the desert, she took off and landed at Baghdad when it was almost dark. Here, for the first time, she found some interest in herself but she was too busy checking *Jason*'s engine to bother about reporters and, early next morning, she was heading down the valley of the Euphrates towards the Persian Gulf.

From Bandar Abbas, where she worked until midnight on her plane, she set off at dawn to cover the last lap to Karachi. This was the sixth day. She had beaten the solo record from London to India by two days and she was already famous.

To her astonishment, she was taken to Government

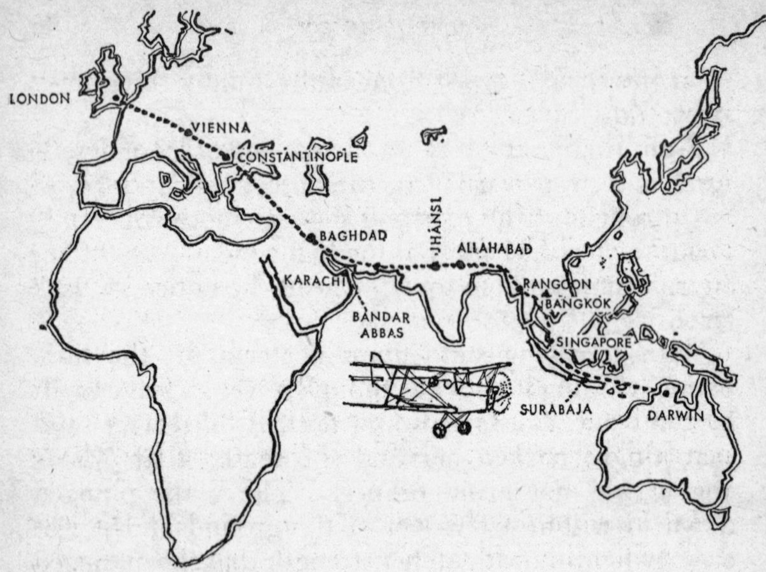


House where she spent the night as guest of honour. A cable arrived from her parents:

'Good Luck. Keep it up. You are doing splendidly. Great interest here in your flight.'

By this time, newspapers were vying with each other to produce front-page photographs of Amy in flying kit, in overalls and as a little girl.

'Next stop, Allahabad!' announced the headlines but, owing to shortage of petrol, Amy had to land at Jhansi in Central India and it was not until the eighth day that she reached Allahabad. After a short stay, she went on to Calcutta where she was still two days ahead of Hinkler's record.

Over Burma, she ran into the monsoon and it seemed impossible that an aircraft could survive. But the little Moth battled its way up to 12,000 feet to cross the Yoma mountains.

'It was like flying through Niagara Falls in a hurricane,' said Amy.

Visibility was so bad when she came down to look for the railway line that, at 150 feet, she could see nothing. Not daring to go lower, she flew blindly to and fro until the steamy mist cleared for an instant to reveal an open space flanked by buildings. It must be Rangoon race-course and, gratefully, she went in to land. *Jason* bumped across a ditch, breaking the propeller and damaging the right wing before coming to rest between a pair of goal-posts. Amy had landed, not at Rangoon, but on a football field ten miles from the city.

Luckily the field was next to a Technical College and willing helpers came out to change the propeller and to fit a new section to the wing. This work took more than a day and then *Jason* had to be taken on a lorry to Rangoon race-course since the field was useless for a take-off.

The next stopping-place was Bangkok, only 350 miles away, or about four hours' flying in good weather. The monsoon closed in and, for seven hours in dense cloud, Amy fought a murderous wind that constantly threatened to dash *Jason* against the mountain slopes.

At half past six, too exhausted to speak, she came down on an airfield of the Siamese Air Force. After a night's sleep, she was away to Singapore where two Moths came up to escort her into the landing-ground.

This was the fourteenth day and the delays had put an end to her hopes of beating Hinkler's record. However, she was still smiling when the R.A.F. drove her to the Officers' Mess for dinner, for *Jason* was being fitted with a new wing for the last lap to Australia.

On the following day, after nine hours' flying, Amy found her petrol so low that she was forced to land in a sugar plantation where the wing fabric was badly torn by some sharp sticks. Although the local people worked furiously to repair the holes, this meant more delay, all the worse because it was going to be very difficult to fly the plane out of a small muddy field.

'There's a much bigger field two miles away,' said the plantation manager.

'If you will have all my luggage taken out of the plane,' she replied, 'I'll have a go.'

The lightened machine just skimmed the trees and came safely down on the new field. Grinning porters soon arrived with the luggage and Amy was off to Surabaja.

By now, millions of people were following the flight almost mile by mile, and when a day and a night passed without news of her progress they imagined that she had crashed.

The Dutch authorities sent out wireless messages to the islands and to ships at sea and two flying-boats were about to take off when a message came in that Amy had landed at an isolated place far from a telephone. A crowd of natives had rushed towards her waving spears but they led her over the hills to a mission church where the Dutch pastor gave her a meal and a room for the night.

After this, the flight across the Timor Sea was easy. Halfway across, she sighted an oil tanker and as she swooped joyously down over its deck, the men waved and the wireless operator was already tapping out the news to Port Darwin.

Aircraft came out to lead her in and, as *Jason* touched down and the Australians came surging towards her, Amy could only say:

'I've done it! I've done it!'

All over the world, newspaper placards bore two words:

'SHE'S THERE.'

The flight had taken nineteen days, nearly four more than Hinkler's but a week less than the *Vimy* bomber. It was a wonderful achievement and the whole of Australia acclaimed the girl from Hull.

There were banquets, speeches and public welcomes. From tiredness or from a misunderstanding with her escort, Amy crashed at Brisbane and, although she was unhurt, *Jason* was wrecked and she had to be taken on by another plane to Sidney where she was to attend the State Ball. Her pilot was a handsome young man named Jim Mollison and, during the flight, he passed Amy a note asking if he might dance with her at the Ball. She agreed but, on the evening, she was surrounded by so many people that she did not catch sight of her pilot. Two years later, when he too was famous, they met again in South Africa and not long afterwards they were married.

By ship and plane, Amy returned to England where

200,000 people came to Croydon to welcome her home. From the air-liner steps, she looked across this vast crowd and there, to her delight, beside the platform where a group of distinguished persons was waiting, stood *Jason* repaired and splendid in a fresh coat of green and white paint!

Through streets lined with cheering crowds, she drove to the Savoy Hotel to receive the *Daily Mail*'s cheque for £10,000 and on to Buckingham Palace to be decorated by King George V.

Amy did not rest on one success. She made a flight to Tokyo, and after her marriage she beat Jim Mollison's record flight from London to the Cape and back, and was the first woman to fly the Atlantic. On this trip, she and her husband were lucky not to be killed when they crashed at night a few miles from New York.

There were many other flights, records and mishaps in her adventurous career. The end came in 1941 when, as a war-time pilot in the Air Transport Auxiliary, her plane broke up in mid-air as she was crossing the Thames estuary. The wreckage fell into the river mud but no trace was ever found of Amy Johnson. As she said herself, her spirit found its outlet in the air. Everything in her life spelt adventure.

# WINSTON CHURCHILL

'If you have any money in your possession, you may hand it over,' said the Headmaster.

He was a large man with an imposing moustache and his manner showed that he expected obedience. The small, freckled boy dug unwillingly into his pockets and produced three halfcrowns that his mother had just given him.

'The School shop is open once a week,' snapped the Headmaster as he placed the money in a drawer.

The boy eyed him with hostility. This was his first day at school; he was only seven and the halfcrowns were a last link with home and his toy-filled nursery. Now they had vanished like the Headmaster's smile when Mother departed.

Presently the boy found himself seated at a battered desk in an empty form-room. A master came in.

'So you're Churchill? Have you done any Latin?'

'No, sir.'

'Here is a Latin grammar. You will learn the first page. I shall come back in half an hour.'

A strange collection of words stared back at the boy:

*Mensa*—a table. *Mensa*—O table.
*Mensam*—a table. *Mensae*—of a table.
*Mensae*—to or for a table.
*Mensa*—by, with or from a table.

It made no sense but the boy had a good memory and when the master returned he gabbled it off correctly.

'That is satisfactory, Churchill.'

'Please, sir, what does it mean?'

'It means what it says. *Mensa*, the Latin word for a table.'

'But what does "O table" mean.'

'That is the vocative case. You would use it when speaking to a table.'

'But I never do!' blurted out the boy.

'If you are impertinent, Churchill, you will be punished—and punished very severely,' replied the master. He was quite right. Punishment was frequent and severe at this expensive school. Two or three times a month, the Headmaster summoned the entire school to listen to the screams of an offender being thrashed until he bled.

Winston Churchill decided that he hated school. He was obstinate and no amount of beating would make him learn things that did not interest him.

'In all the twelve years I was at school, no one

ever succeeded in making me write a Latin verse,' he said.

After a time his father, Lord Randolph Churchill, noticed that his son was making no progress.

'Winston's reports are very bad,' he remarked to his wife. 'We had better find another school.'

They did so at Brighton. It was a smaller, kindlier place where Winston enjoyed French, History, lots of poetry and, above all, swimming and riding, but his behaviour was far from perfect.

'A small red-headed pupil, the naughtiest boy in the class,' reported one of his teachers.

At the age of twelve, Winston had to take the Entrance Examination for Harrow. His father was a successful politician and his mother was one of the most fascinating women in England. The Churchills knew or were related to nearly everyone of importance and it was naturally expected that their eldest son would be as brilliant as his parents.

Yet, faced with the Latin paper at Harrow, Winston could do no more than write his name at the top of the page. There was not a single question that he could answer.

However, the Headmaster admitted him and placed him in the lowest form. Since Latin, Greek and Mathematics were the most prized subjects at Harrow and Winston loathed all three, he stayed at the bottom of the school for a very long time.

'But I *was* taught English,' he said cheerfully. 'We were considered such dunces that we could only learn English!'

At least he won a prize. This was for reciting over a thousand lines of poetry without a mistake and he also won the Public Schools' Championship for fencing. But, to most people and to his father, he was a merry, truculent little chap, the dunce of a famous family.

One day, in the holidays, Lord Randolph found Winston and his brother Jack in the old nursery. Winston had fifteen hundred toy-soldiers, besides forts, artillery and transports and the game was being played with such skill that Lord Randolph watched for twenty minutes. Then he said:

'Would you like to go into the Army, Winston?'

The boy looked up eagerly. He would do anything to please this great man, to prove that he was not really a dunderhead.

'Yes, Father,' he answered.

'We'll have to see if you can get into Sandhurst,' said his father, adding under his breath, 'You'll never make a lawyer as I had hoped.'

At the third attempt, Winston entered Sandhurst as a cavalry-cadet. Even this did not please his father.

'I hoped you would pass high enough for the infantry,' he snorted. 'The cavalry is expensive. Horses, grooms and uniforms are most costly and, from what I can see, there is every prospect of you turning into a waster!'

Poor Winston! He never managed to impress his father, for within a short while Lord Randolph died at the early age of forty-five.

At Sandhurst, Winston took subjects that interested him—tactics, map-making, gymnastics and riding. For the first time he worked hard, and by the end of his year he passed out eighth of his batch of 150 cadets. He was gazetted to the 4th Hussars.

It was a glorious thing to be a cavalry officer in 1895 and Winston was thrilled by the hard training, the glittering jingle of men and horses, the excitement of manoeuvring at a gallop. In addition, because of his name and his mother's position in Society, he was able to enjoy himself as a dashing young man-about-town.

The only disappointment was the lack of adventure. The British Army had not fought a serious war for almost forty years and the one place in the world where shots were being fired in anger was Cuba. A guerrilla war was going on between the local rebels and their Spanish rulers, so, through family influence, Winston obtained permission to go to Cuba as an observer.

On his 21st birthday, in the Cuban forest, he heard for the first time the crack of gunfire and the whistle of bullets. It was immensely exciting and, to his surprise, rather less dangerous than he had thought.

Home from this first taste of adventure, Winston found that his regiment was posted to India where the cavalry settled down to the usual routine of parades and polo.

Winston was bored. He loved polo but his mind was too active to enjoy idleness and he almost began to wish that he had not wasted his time at Harrow.

'It's not too late,' he said to himself. 'I always liked history at school. I will start with history.'

He wrote to ask his mother to send out some books. Box upon box of thick heavy volumes arrived at his bungalow. He had no idea there was so much learning in the world and he began to read.

'All through the long glistening middle hours of the Indian day, from when we quitted stables to the hour of Polo, I devoured Gibbon,' he wrote. 'I enjoyed it all. I went on to Macaulay . . . I read for four or five hours every day—history, philosophy and a great deal more.'

After two years of this 'curious education', Churchill heard that a rebellion had broken out on the Indian frontier. He was off like a shot. Having wangled leave from his regiment, he made north and joined the Malakand Field Force as correspondent to an English newspaper. This would help his expenses since, even with £500 a year from his mother, he was finding it impossible to live on his pay.

Lieutenant Churchill was soon toiling up the side of a rocky valley with a small party that was to capture a village of mud huts. The resistance was so fierce that they were ordered to retire. Several men were hit and, since it was a point of honour never to leave wounded men to be tortured to death, Churchill, the Adjutant and several soldiers went back to rescue them.

'We were not halfway across the open space when thirty or forty furious figures appeared firing frantically and waving their swords . . . I looked to my left . . . the Adjutant had been shot . . . the leading tribesman rushed upon his prostrate body and slashed it three or four times with his sword. I forgot everything except a desire to kill this man . . . I pulled out my revolver and fired. No result. I fired again. No

result. I fired again. Whether I hit him or not, I cannot tell. At any rate, he ran back and plumped down behind a rock. I looked round. I was alone with the enemy.'

In a rain of bullets, he reached his friends behind a knoll. Just when it seemed certain that they would be wiped out, the Buffs arrived and the tribesmen were driven off.

Churchill saw some more action before being recalled to his regiment and, by this time, he had decided to write a book about the campaign. Called *The Story of the Malakand Field Force*, it was praised in the Press and by the Prime Minister and the Prince of Wales. There were other opinions.

'Who the devil does this conceited whipper-snapper think he is?' exploded one colonel. 'How dare he criticize Her Majesty's senior officers!'

Thus, when Churchill tried to join General Kitchener's Staff in the Sudan, Kitchener refused to have him at any price. Nothing daunted, Churchill got himself attached to the 21st Lancers without pay. He cheerfully agreed that if he got killed in the forthcoming campaign, there must be no claim on Army funds!

The 21st Lancers joined Kitchener's army just before the battle of Omdurman and were ordered to head off the enemy's right flank.

'Talk about fun!' wrote Churchill. 'On horseback, at daybreak, within shot of an advancing army . . .'

The trumpet sounded 'Right wheel into line' and 300 lancers swung round and broke into a gallop.

Because of a dislocated shoulder, Churchill sheathed his sword and drew his pistol. The lancers swept through the Dervish riflemen and plunged unexpectedly into a dry water-course among 3000 of the enemy. They were instantly engulfed by a mass of tribesmen who fearlessly slashed at horses and men. Churchill fired, straightened himself in the saddle and rode so hard at a figure with an uplifted sword that his pistol struck the man's chest. He aimed at an Arab horseman in a steel helmet and suddenly was through and clear. He reined his horse and looked for his troop. He found them re-forming, the enemy made off and one of the last cavalry charges in history was over.

Soon after Omdurman, Churchill went home. He had made three decisions. Since he could not live on his pay, he would leave the Army. He would earn his living as a writer. He would enter Parliament.

Thus, in 1899, brimful of confidence and energy, he was writing a book about the recent campaign and was standing as Conservative candidate at Oldham. To his astonishment, the electors did not choose him but actually preferred Mr. Runciman, a Liberal.

'Never mind,' said Mr. Runciman to his disappointed rival, 'I don't suppose the world has heard the last of either of us!'

A number of influential people already knew that 'the little square-headed fellow' had dash and a ready wit, but he was not yet known to the general public. He became a hero through a series of accidents.

The Boer War broke out soon after the Oldham election and Churchill went to South Africa as a newspaper correspondent. He arrived to find that the Boers were besieging Mafeking, Kimberley and Ladysmith. From Durban, he could get no farther along the railway than the little town of Estcourt.

Here he met Captain Haldane, an old friend who offered to take him in an armoured-train that patrolled a stretch of line towards besieged Ladysmith.

'Nothing looks more impressive than an armoured-train,' wrote Churchill, 'but nothing is more vulnerable and helpless. It was only necessary to blow up a bridge to leave the monster stranded, far from home and at the mercy of the enemy.'

The train, carrying 120 soldiers armed with rifles, consisted of an engine and six trucks, three in front and three behind. This moving fort had puffed along for fourteen miles when a party of Boers was sighted near the line. The order was given to return home. As bullets and shrapnel tanged against the steel-sided trucks, the driver put on speed, rounded a bend and crashed into a huge boulder placed on the line. The three trucks, now in front, were overturned, two falling clear but the third lay half on, half off the track.

Many of the soldiers were badly injured but those in the rear trucks under Captain Haldane returned the Boers' fire while Churchill went along the track to survey the damage and to get the injured under cover.

After an hour's work, he realized that the best hope was to uncouple the rear trucks and to direct the engine-driver to butt and pull the obstruction. At last, with a rasping screech, the engine scraped by. The way home was clear if he could recouple the rear trucks.

Haldane was engaged so hotly that it was impossible to spare men to move the trucks.

'Get the wounded on to the engine, Churchill,' he shouted. 'I'll bring my men along on foot.'

Crammed with wounded men, the engine moved slowly forward while the rest of the soldiers marched alongside, sheltering from the shells and bullets as best they could. On a slope, the engine began to get ahead of the soldiers who became fully exposed to the enemy fire. Churchill jumped down and ran back to bring along Haldane at a faster pace.

In a cutting, he saw two men with rifles. They were Boers. He turned and scrambled up the bank as their bullets hissed past him. He was over and making for shelter when he found himself covered by the rifle of a seated horseman. He put his hand to his belt but his revolver was gone. When clearing the line, he had put it down in the engine-cab. The Boer looked along the sights of his rifle and Churchill ruefully surrendered. He was taken to where Haldane and his men had been captured and, with sixty others, he was soon on his way to Pretoria.

Formerly a school, the prisoner-of-war camp was surrounded by a wall patrolled by sentries, and at night the entire area was brightly lit by electric lamps. While he was considering various ways of escape, Churchill noticed that one part of the wall was in shadow and that it might just be reached from a lavatory built alongside.

One evening he strolled across the yard and hid himself in the lavatory. Through a chink he watched two sentries some fifteen yards away until, after an age, they turned their backs and began to talk.

'Now or never!' he said to himself. Jumping up, he gripped the top of the wall and heaved himself over. For one horrible moment, his waistcoat became caught in some ironwork, he freed it and dropped down into a shrubbery.

There was still a sentry to pass outside but, jamming a civilian hat on his head, Churchill strolled past him, whistling a tune and deliberately walking in the middle of the road.

The streets were full of people but no one took any notice of a short figure in a brown suit who sat down by a bridge to consider his next move. He was in the heart of the enemy country, without a map or a compass. All he knew was that Delagoa Bay in Portuguese East Africa lay about 300 miles to the east so he had better find the railway and follow that.

Presently, he struck the railway and began to walk

briskly along the track. After two hours, he came to a station and hid himself in a ditch. A train drew in, waited a few minutes and began to pull out, gathering speed faster than he expected. He hurled himself forward, missed, clutched again and hung on until he pulled himself on to the coupling of a truck.

Just before dawn, he jumped off the train, quenched his thirst in a pool of water and lay up in a wood to await another train that night. The day crawled by and when darkness fell, he returned to the line in high hopes. Hours passed but no train came along so he set off on foot.

Dozens of detours were necessary to avoid guards at bridges and stations. He fell into swamps, waded across streams and was becoming exhausted when he sighted what seemed to be the fires of a native village. The Kaffirs, he understood, hated the Boers and might be willing to help an Englishman so he stumbled on towards the lights. They proved to be the fires not of a village but of some furnaces. He had come to a coal mine.

All through his life, in critical situations that called for a sudden decision, Churchill put his faith in Providence and his own courage. Taking a deep breath, he knocked on the door of the colliery house.

An upper window opened and a voice called out.

'I want help,' answered Churchill. 'I have had an accident. I have fallen off a train.'

A man came to the door. He was holding a revolver.

'Well, come in,' he said suspiciously.

Indoors, the man lit a lamp and surveyed his grimy exhausted visitor. 'I think I'd like to know a bit more about this accident,' he said slowly.

'I think I'd better tell you the truth,' replied Churchill.

When he had finished, the man got up and locked the door. Then he held out his hand.

'This is the only house for twenty miles where you would not be handed over. We're British here and we'll see you through.'

He was John Howard, manager of the Transvaal Colliery and, with a few others, the Boers had let him stay on to keep the mine in working order. But it was dangerous for him to offer help, especially as there were Dutch servant-girls sleeping in the house.

'It must be done. We'll manage

it somehow,' he muttered as he fetched bread and meat for his famished guest.

Before daylight, he lowered Churchill into the mine where two Scots led him to a disused shaft. There, with only rats for company, he spent the next few days while the Boers scoured the district, offering a reward for Churchill's capture, dead or alive.

Meanwhile, Mr. Howard was making plans to smuggle the fugitive on to a train leaving for Delagoa Bay. In a narrow space between huge bales of wool covered by a tarpaulin, Churchill jolted eastwards for three days. At last, through a crack, he saw the uniforms of Portuguese officials. He waited until the train moved on and then, unable to restrain his joy, he stuck his head out of the tarpaulin, sang and

crowed at the top of his voice and fired Mr. Howard's pistol into the air!

At Delagoa Bay, the British Consul put him on a steamer to Durban where he was greeted by a big crowd and a brass band. After a series of defeats, Churchill's escape gave the British something to cheer about and although he said himself that the whole affair was exaggerated, it brought him fame and he was not the man to waste his good fortune.

Within a month he was an unpaid officer in the South African Light Horse and had taken part in a sharp fight at Spion Kop. After this he entered Ladysmith when the town was relieved, marched 500 miles with Lord Roberts' army and cycled into Johannesburg while it was still in Boer hands.

In October 1900, exactly one year after he had set off to South Africa, he was elected to Parliament for Oldham, defeating the same Mr. Runciman by 230 votes. The world had heard of him sooner than even he had expected!

For the next sixty years Churchill's career was more brilliant and stormy than his father's had been. He left the Conservatives to join the Liberals, served under Lloyd George and, as First Lord of the Admiralty, he had the Fleet ready and at sea when the Great War broke out in 1914.

A year later, his plan to shorten the war by attacking Turkey was a failure and he left the Government to become a serving-officer in France. After the war, the Conservatives would not forgive him for deserting them and all through the thirties he was out of office and out of favour. His career seemed to be over.

In adversity, Churchill never lost his courage and

sense of fun. He devoted himself to writing history and, having picked up a child's box of paints by chance, he became such a colourful painter that several of his pictures were hung in the Royal Academy. Visitors to his home in Kent often found him in the gardens that he had laid out and, chuckling with pride, he would show them the garden wall he had built himself.

In Parliament and in the newspapers, he was never silent. Year in and year out, he warned the country of Germany's rising strength and Hitler's violent ambition. People scoffed at his constant talk of danger. 'A brilliant failure. An old war-monger,' they said.

But in 1939, when Germany attacked Poland, he was given his old post at the Admiralty and a message went round the Fleet, 'Winston's back!' In 1940 he became Prime Minister.

France fell. The Germans crushed western Europe and although the British army escaped from Dunkirk, all its arms and equipment were lost. The country was on the brink of complete defeat. Was it not sensible to ask for peace, to make terms even with Hitler?

The country asked for leadership and Churchill spoke:

'I have nothing to offer but blood, toil, tears and sweat . . . You ask what is our policy? I will tell you, it is to wage war, by sea, by land and air, with all our might and with all the strength that God can give us. You ask what is our aim? I can answer in one word: Victory.'

But what if Britain was invaded? The Germans were massing their armies on the French coast and the British had not enough rifles to go round. Churchill gave the answer:

'We shall defend our island, whatever the cost may be, we shall fight on the beaches, we shall fight on the landing-grounds, we shall fight in the fields and in the streets, we shall fight in the hills, we shall never surrender.'

The words of one 'little square-headed fellow' rallied the nation. But more than words were needed in the years of bombing at home and of disasters overseas.

By his courage, hard work and unflagging confidence in victory, Churchill inspired his people and heartened his allies. At an age when most men are growing old, he showed superhuman ability to do without sleep, to see into every part of the war effort, to travel thousands of miles to meet allied leaders and to see the troops in the field. Only the king's protest stopped him from joining the landings at Normandy! Always he seemed to be the voice of his own people, expressing their anger and pity, their stubborn will to go on to the end.

Once, during the bombing of London, he was interviewed by an American as he stood among the ruins of homes of ordinary people:

'They deserve victory,' he growled, 'and by God they shall have it!'

Victory came at last and he was in Germany conferring with Stalin and the American President when he learnt that he was no longer Prime Minister. The people had voted for a Labour government and Mr. Attlee took his place.

Churchill was over seventy but he returned to lead the Conservatives and to write a magnificent six-volume history of the war. In 1951 he was Prime Minister again until, at the age of eighty, he decided to retire, but not to rest. He went on writing, painting and travelling all over the world.

In his long adventurous career, Winston Churchill suffered defeats and disappointments. He was rash, he made mistakes and sometimes he was unfair to his opponents. But, if he had faults, he had the gift of leadership. He was the greatest Englishman of our time.

He died in 1965 and was given a State Funeral. The only other commoner to receive this honour was Wellington in 1852.

## LEONARD CHESHIRE, V.C.

'Everything's O.K., Captain, except Taffy's intercom.'

'Where are we, Desmond?'

'Between Wesseling and Cologne.'

'We'll go for Cologne. Tell Taffy to aim for the marshalling-yards.'

The captain remembered that Davidson, the wireless operator was making his first trip.

'You all right, Davey?'

'Fine, thank you, sir.'

'Good lad. We'll want your flares in five minutes.'

'I think there's a fighter behind us, Captain.'

'O.K., Revs, keep an eye on him. We're almost up to Cologne now. Taffy ready?'

'Bombs fused! Bomb doors open!'

'Left, left, about 20 degrees.'

'Look out! Turn quick! Over . . . !'

A violent explosion rocked the aircraft and caused it to plunge downwards. Blinded by the brilliant flash, half-choked by smoke, the pilot fought for control. His mind raced over the things he must do; he wondered how the crew was behind, cursed himself for not having put on his oxygen mask, for forgetting where he had thrown his parachute.

Pull the stick back. Steady, steady. That's better, smoke clearing, can see the instruments. All haywire but the altimeter says 5000 feet. Not bad. Level out.

Behind him, a voice cried:

'Fire! The tank's on fire!'

'Well put it out!' he snapped.

The Whitley wallowed and flopped. The port wing dropped but the pilot stopped her spinning as more shells came up from the German guns. A searchlight caught the damaged bomber, then another, but he dared not take violent evasive action so he flew straight and level, hoping for the best.

His back felt hot and, half-turning, he could see red streaks of fire. There was an awful smell of rubber burning and sounds of slapping and cursing. The second pilot appeared alongside him.

'Hello, Desmond. How's the fire?'

'Taffy's got it under control. There's a blooming great hole in our side. Can you keep her going?'

'Of course. Have we still got the bombs?'

'Yes, we have.'

'Well we'd better find Cologne and drop 'em.'

Another figure appeared on the step. His face was a blackened burnt mask with blood-filled circles where his eyes had been. It was Davey. When the shell hit the Whitley, it had ignited the flare he was about to drop. On fire, he had pushed it out and also the second flare that would have exploded and destroyed the plane. The others had beaten out the flames before tackling the fire under a petrol tank.

'You'll want a fix, sir. I won't let you down, I must get back to the wireless, but I can't see, sir, I can't see.'

Revs took him back to his set. Freezing air through

the hole in the Whitley's side was agonizing to the burnt boy but he talked only about his wireless set. Unable to see, he told Revs how to set the dials, got him to guide his hands to the key and refused to give up until he collapsed. Revs wrapped him in his own flying jacket and held him like a child, while the others fixed up a parachute for him. There was no parachute for Revs.

The damaged Whitley flew doggedly on and crossed the English coast at Cromer. It was growing light when they touched down at Base where the waiting ground-crew gazed at the smashed fuselage.

'Blimey!' said an awed voice, 'it's only half a kite!'

The captain was last out.

'Steady with Davey,' he said to the stretcher-bearers as he saw his wireless-op. into the ambulance.

The official account of that episode in 1940 announced the award of the Distinguished Flying Medal to Sergeant Davidson and the D.S.O. to Pilot Officer Cheshire. To his indignation he learned that for Desmond, Taffy and Revs, there was nothing.

Leonard Cheshire was twenty-three when he

became captain of the Whitley bomber. A slight, oval-faced young man, he had joined Oxford University Air Squadron just before the war when, as a wild law-student, he was looking for thrills more amusing than racing his red sports-car through the Oxfordshire lanes. War came and Cheshire was trained for bombers.

'I was never what you would call a good pilot,' he said. 'My cockpit drill was terrible . . . always hated it . . . And if I left off flying for more than a day, then I flew shockingly. But I was lucky. Everyone knew I was lucky.'

To survive, a pilot had to be lucky, no matter how good he was. Every single one of the friends with whom he flew in those days was killed or missing—Lofty, his first captain, Desmond, Willy, Jimmy, Christopher, his brother, Taffy, Revs—but Cheshire stayed alive. Night after night, he went out into the darkness towards Germany—to Cologne, Essen, Duisberg, Berlin, and Berlin again—and he always came back.

From Whitleys he moved to four-engined Halifaxes and had to master new equipment. So, on non-flying

days, he would blindfold himself and move around inside his plane teaching himself to find every knob and panel by touch. He would talk to his ground-crew and ask their advice about engines and gun-turrets before taking them out for a drink.

'He gave us all the feeling that we were important and could be trusted and I'll never forget what that trust meant,' said Aircraftman Laurie Scott.

At the end of his first operational tour Cheshire was awarded the D.F.C. and was sent by sea to the United States on special duty. The Americans, not yet in the war, gave a terrific welcome to British airmen and 'Chesh' basked in the bright light of fame and gay parties before flying a Hudson back to England.

By 1943 he was Wing-Commander Cheshire commanding 76 Squadron and, besides his other missions, he had taken part in seven raids on Berlin. The strain told on his health and beneath his jaunty charm he was moody and irritable. Awarded a second D.S.O., he was taken off flying and promoted Group Captain, at twenty-five, the youngest who had yet reached that rank.

He soon became bored with the duties of a Station Commander. To him, war meant flying against the enemy, not training other people to do so or sitting in an office signing papers. But it was far from easy to get back into the air when some of his senior officers considered him an odd character, too much of a showman for their liking. In any case, it seemed as if his nerves had cracked up.

Intelligence picked up information about a new German weapon, a long-range rocket bomb known as the V2 that was intended to wipe out London. When Mr. Churchill gave orders that Bomber Command must attack the launching-sites, Cheshire managed to persuade his superiors to give him the chance he had been longing for.

Dropping to the rank of Wing-Commander, he took over the famous Dam-buster Squadron 617, whose Lancasters were specially equipped for attacking the heavily-guarded sites. The Germans had built rocket-shelters covered by thirty feet of concrete and it was difficult to hit, let alone to penetrate, such targets. An 'earthquake bomb' weighing 12,000 pounds was produced that needed to be dropped so expertly that it would sink into the earth alongside the shelters and explode under the foundations. From a great height this was impossible, so Cheshire practised low-flying in a fast Mosquito in order to place a marker bomb for the Lancasters, 20,000 feet above.

He gave the credit for this success to Mick Martin, a brilliant Australian pilot:

'I learned all I know of this low-flying game from Mick. I never saw him make a mistake.'

Rocket-sites, explosives factories, E-boat pens were successfully attacked. After a time Cheshire asked for an American Mustang, a single-engined fighter that was faster than the Mosquito. Acting as his own navigator, bomb-aimer and wireless operator, he would dive the Mustang through a hail of shrapnel to drop his marker at the last second and flatten out just above the guns.

Altogether, Cheshire led 617 Squadron on forty raids and he had made exactly one hundred trips when he was called to Group Headquarters.

'I see that you've done a hundred trips,' said Air Vice-Marshal Cochrane. 'That's enough. It's time you had a rest.'

Cheshire began to protest. The A.V.M. looked at him keenly, noticing his thinness and the fact that one eye twitched all the time.

'It's no good arguing,' he said quietly. 'A hundred's a good number to stop at.'

For leadership and courage, Cheshire was awarded the Victoria Cross and as he left Buckingham Palace he was surrounded by the Press reporters:

'My V.C. was given me not for anything I did but for all of 617 Squadron,' he snapped. 'Lots of other chaps deserved them more than I did.'

When the Allies were able to turn all their strength against Japan, Group-Captain Cheshire was sent to America where an explosive of fantastic power had been produced. Since President Truman had decided to use this atomic bomb against Japan, the British Government insisted on British observers being present. Two only could go, a scientist, Dr. Penny and an R.A.F. officer, Group-Captain Cheshire.

Thus, on August 9th, 1945, Cheshire was seated in the nose of an American B.29 Super-Fortress bomber, flying at 39,000 feet towards the city of Nagasaki. Seated comfortably in a warm pressurized atmosphere, he could not help smiling a little at the tremendous excitement of the American crew. Of course, he knew that it was a very important bomb they were carrying but this was armchair stuff compared with those freezing nights over Germany. He grinned across at Dr. Penny. These scientist-chaps had been talking about millions of degrees of heat—well, he had seen a few explosions in his time and figures didn't mean much when people talked in millions. They must be over Japan now. No gunfire, not a sign of fighters anywhere.

'Glasses on, everyone!'

Cheshire put on his pair of thick dark glasses and, at that instant, the bomber was lit by a searing flash fiercer than the very heart of the sun. Appalled by its brightness, Cheshire looked back and saw a gigantic ball of fire soaring upwards drawing with it a trail of smoke that rose in a colossal pillar and spread slowly into a mushroom-shaped cloud.

Although he did not yet know that this single bomb had ripped a city away from the surface of the earth, destroying 40,000 people in a split second, Cheshire sensed that he had witnessed one of the most disastrous events in history. He realized that man had made

a bomb that could destroy not a city or a country but life itself. Somehow, he had had a share in this. From now on, the world was changed and Cheshire was a changed man.

After the war, life in England seemed very dull and Cheshire, who had left the R.A.F., longed for the fun and excitement of Service life.

Why shouldn't ex-service men and women form groups to work together for the good of all? He asked the question through a newspaper and 200 enthusiasts joined his scheme.

'We'll take over a disused aerodrome or a big estate,' he told them. 'Everyone will contribute a sum of money to get started and then we'll farm the land and follow our trades to make ourselves self-supporting. Everyone will have an equal share.'

The first colony started with enthusiasm and it failed because people were selfish and argumentative. Cheshire did not give up easily. He opened another colony at Le Court in Hampshire, an estate that he bought cheaply from an aunt. Its chances of success seemed to be quite bright and he went off to raise funds in Canada but, in his absence, the colony fell to pieces. To pay its debts, he had to sell the land and he was about to close down the big, shabby house when he heard about Arthur Dykes.

Arthur, an ex-airman, had been one of the early colonists but he was now in hospital suffering from cancer. The matron told Cheshire that his case was hopeless. He was alone, with no relatives or money and his hospital bed was urgently wanted.

'I'll take you back to Le Court, if you'll risk it,' said Cheshire.

The big house was empty for everything had been sold but Cheshire borrowed a bed and blankets and carried Arthur into a room that he had cleaned and decorated himself. At least he had found himself a job.

'Life became pretty full,' he said. 'When I wasn't looking after Arthur and cooking meals, I was scything grass and tidying the place up. It was at night we used to talk. Arthur was a Roman Catholic and he used to talk about religion. Then, before he went to sleep, he would read for a bit—always the same book.'

As Arthur grew weaker, Cheshire had to do everything for him. At first, he knew little about nursing but he would ring up the hospital and charm the matron and nurses into telling him what to do:

'You see, I must look after this chap,' he would say. 'There's no one else.'

Nor was there anyone else to look after the old Cockney woman of ninety, bedridden and deaf, whom he took into Le Court. She was his second patient and he became very fond of her, even if he had to do battle to get her bedsocks off every time he washed her!

Arthur died quietly, still holding his book. Cheshire took it gently from him and looked at its title, *One Lord, One Faith*. He started to read.

He had been trying to live a Christian life, to do some good through the colonies and Le Court and, ever since Nagasaki, he had thought a lot about God. Now it seemed as if Arthur had left him the answer to so many of his questions; he spoke to the priest who used to visit Arthur and, after months of instruction, he was received into the Roman Catholic Church.

At Le Court the work went on. By 1949 there were over thirty patients, many suffering from incurable illnesses. Some were old, some were crippled and all of them needed help. In the 'family' that Cheshire created, they learned that most could do something for themselves and for the others.

'He just took in anyone who knocked at the door,' said one of his helpers, for by now there was a band of friends who scrubbed floors, peeled vegetables and nursed the sick.

Cheshire became ill simply because he would not stop working, and with difficulty his friends persuaded him to leave the Home in their care while he took up some other occupation for a time.

He went back to flying as a civilian pilot and he was testing secret equipment in Cornwall when, from the air, he noticed a group of old R.A.F. huts.

'Just the place for another Home,' he declared. At the aerodrome people scoffed at the idea:

'There's no heating or sanitation. The huts have been used as cowsheds and the whole place is derelict. The fellow's crazy.'

'I'll tell you something I've just found out,' remarked a test-pilot thoughtfully. 'You remember Hilda, the little grey-haired woman who works in the canteen? Well, she fell ill some weeks ago and was dying in some wretched cottage with no one to look after her. Cheshire went along and, against all regulations, smuggled her into his own quarters and nursed her until she was better. They say she worships the ground he walks on.'

There was silence. Then an engineer spoke.

'Crazy or not, I reckon the bloke's a saint. If he wants to mend those huts, let's give him a hand.'

With the cheerful assistance of men from a nearby naval air-station, they laid floors, mended roofs and put in stoves and window-panes. When the first patient arrived, an ex-Frogman suffering from T.B., the second 'Cheshire Home', St. Teresa's, was ready.

'My son is mentally ill and I can no longer manage

him. As he was a bomber pilot, I think that he might listen to you. Please will you help me?'

Cheshire read this anguished letter and wrote immediately:

'I will take him into St. Teresa's.'

When the man proved to be so difficult that he upset the other patients, Cheshire decided that he must open another home for men whose minds and nerves were broken. Called Holy Cross it stands near to St. Teresa's.

Ceaseless work and several bouts of influenza made him so tired that his priest advised him to rest. Cheshire's reply was to work harder than ever until, quite suddenly, he collapsed.

Examination showed that he was suffering from tuberculosis of the lungs and, from hospital in Cornwall, he was taken to a sanatorium in Sussex where he had several severe operations.

Two years in bed gave him time to think and to deluge his friends with new ideas. Before his illness, he had meant to start a crusade to take religion to people who never went to church. He obtained some second-hand buses and, since he could not leave his bed, his supporters drove the buses round the streets and played recordings of his voice to attract people to listen and to enter his 'churches on wheels'.

Another of his ideas was to charter planes to take sick people to the Shrine at Lourdes in France where many miraculous cures have taken place and on his first weekend from the sanatorium he himself went there with a drainage tube in his chest.

Meanwhile, the Cheshire Homes still filled his mind. Le Court was rebuilt by the Carnegie Trust to become a place for the care of young people who are ill or crippled. St. Teresa's was enlarged; a new Home, St. Cecilia's, opened in Kent and there are now more than a score of others in various parts of Britain, India, Malaya and Africa. They are there to relieve suffering. Cheshire's work goes on.

## MORE ABOUT THE PEOPLE IN THIS BOOK

ROBERT OWEN (1771–1858) is often called 'the father of British Socialism' because he put forward so many ideas to improve the lives of working people. After he left New Lanark to found new communities in America and elsewhere, people came to look on him as a crank. Most of his projects failed; he spent his fortune and died almost poor at Newtown but he was never bitter and the workers continued to revere his name. He was a pioneer ahead of his time and most of his ideas—nursery schools, state education, decent housing, national insurance, trade unions and planned towns—are accepted today without argument.

ARTHUR, DUKE OF WELLINGTON (1769–1852) was only forty-six at the time of the Battle of Waterloo. He lived to be eighty-three, to play a leading part in politics and to become Prime Minister. His opposition to the Reform Bill of 1832 made him very unpopular and his windows were broken by the London mob. He despised public opinion, danger, show and extravagance, but as he grew old he came to be regarded with enormous respect. Although there was a gay side to his nature, he was a lonely man and his marriage was not happy. Unlike Napoleon and Nelson, he was always modest about his own career and said that he would die to prevent the people suffering the horrors of war. He died at Walmer Castle where his bare, plain room may be seen unchanged.

ELIZABETH GARRETT ANDERSON (1836–1917) built up a large practice among the London poor for whom she opened St. Mary's Dispensary, and she helped to found the New Hospital for Women and the London School of Medicine for Women. She found time to study for a doctor's degree of Paris University and passed its examination in the French language! While she was physician to a children's hospital she met James Anderson, a ship-owner, and they were married in 1871. When nearly seventy, Elizabeth went back to live in Aldeburgh and became its Mayor, the first woman mayor in Britain.

ROBERT STEPHENSON SMYTH BADEN-POWELL (1857–1941) was born in London, the sixth son of Professor Baden Baden Powell, an Oxford mathematician who died when Robert was three. Known to his family as 'Ste', B-P was educated at Charterhouse and he entered the Army in 1876. During his life he wrote over thirty books, mostly for soldiers and Boy Scouts, besides innumerable articles and stories. He could have been a journalist, actor or artist but he succeeded in giving more happiness and idealism to young people than perhaps anyone who has lived in modern times. In 1929 he became Lord Baden-Powell of Gilwell and in 1937 he was awarded the Order of Merit.

WILLIAM RICHARD MORRIS, later LORD NUFFIELD (1877–1963) was the eldest son of Frederick Morris who had various jobs in farming and offices; he was asthmatic and William, who wanted to be a surgeon, realized that he would have to be the family's main support. He was not an inventor but a born engineer with a flair for business and his fortune came from mass-production of cheap reliable cars. Always a difficult man to work for, irritable, touchy and often petty, he had the gifts of a leader who could win loyalty and high endeavour from those who served him. By the time of his death, his gifts totalled about £30 million and the work of the Nuffield Foundation will go on for generations.

AMY JOHNSON (1905–1941) was one of the small band of pilots whose exploits led to the founding of regular air services throughout the world. Besides Alan Cobham, Byrd, Lindbergh, Kingsford-Smith and Bert Hinkler, there were a few well-known women flyers including Lady Bailey, Amelia Earhart of America and Jean Batten of New Zealand. Amy's greatest achievement was in 1936 when she beat the outward and homeward records to the Cape. Her marriage to Jim Mollison ended in 1938 and she resumed her maiden name and took up gliding and motor-racing before becoming a ferry pilot. After her death the Amy Johnson Scholarship was founded to assist girls to train for careers in aviation.

WINSTON LEONARD SPENCER CHURCHILL (1874–1965) was born at Blenheim Palace, built in honour of his ancestor, John Churchill, Duke of Marlborough. His boyhood was not happy for he felt neglected by his parents both of whom he adored. He was devoted to Mrs. Everard, his nurse, and continued to visit her after he was grown-up. During his long and stormy career. Churchill held almost every important office in the Government but his fame rests chiefly upon his leadership of Britain during the Second World War. However, if he had done nothing else in his life, he would have made a name as a writer, a historian and perhaps as a painter.

LEONARD CHESHIRE (1917– ) was born at Chester, the elder son of an Oxford professor. From Stowe School he went to Oxford to read law. His liking for fast cars, betting and night-clubs got him into various scrapes but he took his degree and entered the R.A.F. in 1939. He became the most celebrated airman of the war not only because of his heroic record as a bomber pilot but because he was a favourite with the Press. Like T. E. Lawrence, he courted publicity yet despised it; he was a man of immense courage with a deeply spiritual nature. In 1959 he married Susan Ryder who had worked in refugee camps, and together, they set up the Ryder-Cheshire Foundation to continue their work for the relief of suffering.

**NATURE DETECTION AND CONSERVATION** *by Jean Mellanby* 25p

552 54019 6

Nature and wild life are today threatened by a variety of man-made dangers such as industrial pollution. This serious problem has baffled our top scientists and politicians. Yet there is plenty that you can do about it, and this book shows how we can all become nature detectives and help preserve wild life, even if we live in the heart of a city. And we can enjoy doing so.

**ALL ABOUT KING ARTHUR** *by Geoffrey Ashe* 30p

552 54039 0 Carousel Non-Fiction

Arthur, King of Britain, became a national hero between the years of 1150–1200. The real ruler during most of that time was Henry II. But the legendary monarch was soon more widely renowned than the actual one . . . and his fame in romance has continued ever since.

How did the Arthurian legend begin, and in what forms have writers and poets presented it over the ages? Even more important are the questions: did King Arthur and his knights ever exist at all? How far are the stories true, how far are they invented? If any of the things happened, when did they happen?

Geoffrey Ashe explores both these paths. He traces the Arthur of fiction from the Middle Ages to the present day; he also tells the historical and archaeological facts of all that is known about the King.

**DISCOVERERS AND ADVENTURERS** *by R. J. Unstead* 30p

552 54031 5 Carousel Non-Fiction

R. J. Unstead has chosen some of the most exciting and intriguing discoverers and adventurers and tells their stories. Among the people he has written about are—John Cabot, who tried to find the North-West Passage, but failed; Lady Jane Grey who was Queen of England for only nine days; John Smith who was the real founder of Virginia; and William Dampier, the famous buccaneer.

**EVERYDAY LIFE IN EARLY IMPERIAL CHINA**
*by Michael Loewe* 35p

552 54043 9 Carousel Non-Fiction

What was it like to live in Imperial China during her first four centuries of greatness 2000 years ago? How did the emperor rule over 50 million inhabitants in over 100 administrative divisions?

Michael Loewe paints a full and vivid picture of the Han period (202 B.C.—A.D. 220). He describes the life of the peasants working the land, as well as the inhabitants of the towns—the rich, the tradesmen and artisans, the courtiers and officials, and the beggars and criminals. He examines their position in society, their work, their stints of government service—either as statutory labourers or in the army, their religious practices, and the elaborate hierarchy of institutions and civil servants who enforced the decisions of the imperial government.

**LOUIS PASTEUR and The Fight Against Disease**
*by Richard Serjeant* 25p

552 54042 0 Carousel Non-Fiction

This book tells the story of Louis Pasteur's many discoveries about disease and the further work that has been done since his death. It also tells the story of Pasteur's life and sets it against the life of his times. This makes clear the problems Pasteur faced, the way he was able to solve them, and the almost unbelievable changes that this brilliant man brought to the world of his day and ours.

**HAVELOK THE WARRIOR** *by Ian Serraillier* 20p

552 52007 1 Carousel Fiction

These are the days when evil men conspired to overthrow the monarchy, greedy for the power and wealth of wearing the crown and ruling the land. The King of Denmark is dead, his son Havelok forced to flee the murderous attempts of Earl Godard by escaping to the shores of England. He grows up to be a great warrior, to recover his kingdom.

**OPERATION SIPPACIK** *by Rumer Godden* 20p

552 52009 8 Carousel Fiction

It took a war to prove the heroism of Sippacik, when she was sent out on a vital mission for the 27th Battery, Royal Artillery, stationed in Cyprus. 'Seytan'—devil—was the name Arif Ali had given her, but to her owner Sippacik was the cleverest donkey in Cyprus. She had to be, she was about to face the enemy. This is her true story.

**THE ARABIAN NIGHTS: ALI BABA AND OTHER STORIES FROM THE THOUSAND AND ONE NIGHTS**

**THE ARABIAN NIGHTS: ALADDIN AND OTHER STORIES FROM THE THOUSAND AND ONE NIGHTS**

*by Amabel Williams-Ellis* 30p

2 Volumes

552 52036 5
552 52037 3 Carousel Fiction

Long ago, there lived a powerful King. His beautiful Queen seemed to love him dearly as he loved her; but one day he discovered that she had been conspiring with his enemies to poison him. Half-mad with rage, this King killed his treacherous Queen and vowed that each time he married, his new wife would be beheaded on the morning after the marriage. For some time the King kept his wicked vow. One day he ordered his Grand Vizier to bring him his eldest daughter, Shahrazad, to be his next Queen. Now Shahrazad was not only beautiful she also knew more than a thousand stories. She devised a plan using these stories to prolong her life and to stop the King fulfilling his vow. These two volumes include some of these tales.

**THE ADVENTURES OF ODD AND ELSEWHERE**

*by James Roose-Evans* 25p

552 52038 Carousel Fiction

Sprawled in a corner, the small bear could see the removal van drive away. Everybody had gone and Odd was left alone in the house. But Odd was not alone for long. Hanging upside done by one leg in a tall cupboard was a circus clown—Elsewhere.

Odd and Elsewhere went to live next door—Fenton House owned by The National Trust—with Collander Moll, the caretaker, and her father Hallelujah Jones, a retired Welsh policeman, who did the garden. One day they went off exploring—and that was the start of all their adventures.

**HERACLES THE STRONG** *by Ian Serraillier* 25p

552 52034 9 Carousel Fiction

Heracles was the son of Zeus, the Father of the gods, but he was born into a mortal family. The goddess Hera hated Heracles because he was not her own, and in a fit of spite and jealousy drove him blindly mad. Like a whirlwind Heracles raged through the palace and committed the most dreadful crimes.

Condemned by the gods, Heracles had no alternative but to accept his punishment and tackle the twelve seemingly impossible tasks set before him by the cowardly King Eurystheus.

## THE HOW AND WHY WONDER BOOK OF EXTINCT ANIMALS 25p

552 86555 9

Here is a fabulous array of animals that have become extinct, from the early dinosaurs to more recent victims of man's actions. And there is also a warning: many species including pandas, tigers and leopards are in danger of disappearing, and the final question posed is 'Is the human race becoming extinct?'

## THE HOW AND WHY WONDER BOOK OF THE SPOILT EARTH 25p

552 86556 7

Pollution is one of the most pressing problems that face the modern world. THE SPOILT EARTH covers the various forms of pollution that threaten our planet, and indeed our everyday life. Only by knowing the facts can we learn how to protect the balance of nature and to build tomorrow's world before it is destroyed.

All these books are available at your bookshop or can be ordered direct from Transworld Publishers Ltd., Cash Sales Dept., P.O. Box 11, Falmouth, Cornwall.

Please send full name and address together with cheque or postal order—no currency and allow 7p per book to cover the cost of postage and packing.

---

If you would like to receive a newsletter telling you about our new children's books, send your name and address to Gillian Osband, Transworld Publishers Ltd., 57/59 Uxbridge Road, Ealing, London, W5, and mention 'CHILDRENS NEWSLETTER'.